MARY MY HOPE

"My Mother, my hope!"

MARY MY HOPE

A MANUAL OF DEVOTION
TO GOD'S MOTHER
AND OURS

By

FATHER LAWRENCE G. LOVASIK, S.V.D.

Divine Word Missionary

NEW REVISED EDITION

CATHOLIC BOOK PUBLISHING CORP.
New Jersey

NIHIL OBSTAT: Joseph P. Penna, J.C.D.

Censor Librorum

IMPRIMATUR: ✠ James P. Mahoney, D.D.

Vicar General, Archdiocese of New York

(T-365)

ISBN 978-0-89942-365-4

CONTENTS

Foreword 11

PART 1

LITURGICAL FEASTS
OF THE BLESSED VIRGIN MARY

Mary, Mother of God, *January* 1 15
Presentation of the Lord, *February* 2 24
Our Lady of Lourdes, *February* 11 33
Annunciation of Our Lord, *March* 25 . . . 41
Visitation, *May* 31 52
Immaculate Heart of Mary 61
Our Lady of Mount Carmel, *July* 16 70
Dedication of St. Mary Major, *Aug.* 5 . . . 76
Assumption of the BVM, *August* 15 83
Queenship of Mary, *August* 22 93
Nativity of the BVM, *September* 8 103
Our Lady of Sorrows, *September* 15 111
Our Lady of the Rosary, *October* 7 120
Presentation of Mary, *November* 21 129
The Immaculate Conception, *Dec.* 8 . . . 135
Our Lady of Guadalupe, *Dec.* 12 143
Nativity of Our Lord, *December* 25 152
Holy Family 161

5

PART 2
PRAYERS OF THE SAINTS
TO OUR LADY

Mary, Vessel of God's Mysteries,
  St. Gregory 172
Mary, Our Hope, *St. Ephrem* 173
Mary, Mother of Grace, *St. Athanasius* .. 173
Mary, Mother of Mercy, *St. Augustine* ... 174
Mary, Mother and Virgin, *St. Cyril* 175
Mary, Life of Christians, *St. Germanus* .. 175
Mary, Hope of Christians,
  St. John Damascene 176
Mary, Beloved of the Trinity,
  St. Francis of Assisi 176
Mary, Queen and Intercessor, *St. Bernard* 177
Mary, Glory of Mothers, *St. Bernard* 178
Mary, Mother of God, *St. Bernard* 178
Dedication to Mary, *St. Thomas Aquinas* 180
For a Happy Death, *St. Bonaventure* 180
Little Psalms to Mary, *St. Bonaventure* .. 180
Favor with God, *St. Albert the Great* 184
Petition to Mary, *St. Gertrude* 184
Offering to Mary, *St. Francis de Sales* ... 185
The Spirit of Mary, *St. Louis de Montfort* 186

Mary, Hope for Salvation,
    St. Alphonsus Liguori 187
Mary, Help of Christians, *St. John Bosco* 188

PART 3

SPECIAL DEVOTIONS TO MARY

Immaculate Mother of God 191
Our Lady of the Miraculous Medal 192
Mediatrix of Grace 193
Immaculate Spouse of the Holy Spirit . . . 194
Our Lady of the Most Blessed Sacrament 195
Immaculate Heart of Mary 196
Mother of Sorrows 198
Mary Assumed into Heaven 199
Mother of Perpetual Help 200
Mother of Mercy 201
Queen of the Rosary 202
Queen of Peace 203

PART 4

GENERAL PRAYERS

Hail, Holy Queen 206
Memorare 206
The Angelus 207

Marian Antiphons:

    Advent-Christmas 207

    Lent 208

    Easter 208

Consecration 209

Consecration of the Family 210

Petition 211

Litany 212

PART 5

THE SCRIPTURAL ROSARY

Pope Paul VI on the Rosary 215

The Holy Rosary 218

The Joyful Mysteries

    The Annunciation 219

    The Visitation 220

    The Birth of Our Lord 221

    The Presentation in the Temple 223

    The Finding in the Temple 224

The Luminous Mysteries

    The Baptism of Jesus 227

    Christ's Self-Manifestation at Cana . . 228

    Christ's Proclamation of the

        Kingdom of God 229

    The Transfiguration 230

    Institution of the Eucharist 231

The Sorrowful Mysteries

> The Agony in the Garden 232
> The Scourging 234
> The Crowning with Thorns 235
> The Carrying of the Cross 237
> The Crucifixion 238

The Glorious Mysteries

> The Resurrection 240
> The Ascension 242
> The Descent of the Holy Spirit 243
> The Assumption of Mary 244
> The Crowning of Mary 246
> Prayer After the Rosary 248

FOREWORD

THE original MARY MY HOPE prayerbook was published in the Marian Year, December 8, 1954, on the occasion of the first centenary of the definition of the dogma of the Immaculate Conception. Over the years the book has enjoyed widespread popularity. After Vatican Council II it was necessary to present devotion to the Blessed Virgin Mary in an updated and new light. Hence the original prayerbook was completely revised.

The material of the new MARY MY HOPE is based on God's Word in the Gospels, the tradition of the Church as expressed by the writings of her saints and scholars, the liturgy, and by her teaching authority voiced by Vatican Council II in the *Constitution on the Church* (November 21, 1964) and by the National Conference of Catholic Bishops of the United States and their *Pastoral Letter on the Blessed Virgin* (November 21, 1973).

Using MARY MY HOPE as a guide will enable the People of God to accompany the Blessed Virgin Mary through the whole liturgical year, admire her spirit, and obtain graces they need to imitate her life of dedication to her Son.

Under the loving care of our Lady I offer
the People of God this new MARY MY
HOPE as a tribute to the Mother of God and
the Mother of the Church. May it be a
means of keeping us close to Mary that we
may the more surely reach her Son!

Father Lawrence S.J.D.

Part 1

LITURGICAL FEASTS
OF THE
BLESSED VIRGIN MARY,
MOTHER OF GOD

—

Doctrine and Prayers

"Mary conceived without sin, pray for us."

FEASTS OF THE
BLESSED VIRGIN MARY

JANUARY

MARY, MOTHER OF GOD

January 1 (Novena: Dec. 24-Jan. 1)

DOCTRINE

AMONG the titles with which faith and love honor the Blessed Virgin Mary, that of "Mother of God" surpasses all others, for in it we find the source and origin of all others. It comprises such praise and glory that no other can be compared with it. The first step toward a recognition of Jesus Christ as Savior of the world is belief in the Divine Maternity.

Mary appears in the first pages of the Gospel as the Mother of Jesus. Her maternal office is mentioned in *the earliest creeds of the Church*. The first symbol listed in the old Roman Creed is: "I believe in God the Father Almighty, and in Christ Jesus His only Son, our Lord, Who was born from the Holy

Spirit and the Virgin Mary, Who was crucified under Pontius Pilate. . . ." This creed appears at the end of the second century, and in its essential content comes from the ages of the Apostles.

The Nicaean Symbol was called forth by the need to defend the divinity of the Son of God. In defending the divinity of the Second Person of the Blessed Trinity, the *Council of Nicaea* (325) was implicitly protecting Mary's privilege as Mother of God.

Nestorius, Archbishop of Constantinople, denied that Mary was the Mother of God and, by a necessary consequence, denied that there was a personal union of the two natures of God and Man in Jesus Christ. Thus the Maternity of Mary involved the whole question of the Incarnation. St. Cyril, Patriarch of Alexandria, presided at the *General Council at Ephesus* in 431 in the name of Pope Celestine. The Council proclaimed: "If anyone should not confess that Emmanuel is truly God, and that in consequence the Blessed Virgin is the Mother of God—for she brought forth according to the flesh the Word of God made flesh—let him be anathema."

The outstanding document of modern times on the divine motherhood is Pius XI's encyclical commemorating the anniversary of Ephesus, *Lux veritatis*, December 25, 1931. In it is explained the central dogma of the Incarnation—that Christ is true God and true man, the divine and human natures existing unconfused in the hypostatic union (the union of the one divine Person with the human nature). The divine Maternity is shown to result from this doctrine.

From all eternity God thought of the Virgin of Nazareth as the future Mother of His Son. At the

Annunciation, Mary became the Mother of God. This is her most exalted title, the source of all her other privileges. On Calvary Christ gave His Mother to all men to be their spiritual Mother, so that through her He came to them. It is the will of Jesus that we love His Mother. We should love her because she is also our Mother.

THE CHURCH SPEAKS

THE Virgin Mary, who at the message of the angel received the Word of God in her heart and in her body and gave Life to the world, is acknowledged and honored as being truly the Mother of God and Mother of the Redeemer. Redeemed by reason of the merits of her Son and united to Him by a close and indissoluble tie, she is endowed with the high office and dignity of being the Mother of the Son of God, by which account she is also the beloved daughter of the Father and the temple of the Holy Spirit. Because of this gift of sublime grace she far surpasses all creatures, both in heaven and on earth.

(Vatican II: *Constitution on the Church*, 53)

In the liturgy "we honor Mary the ever-virgin Mother of Jesus Christ our Lord and God" (Eucharistic Prayer I; "Mary, the virgin Mother of God" (Prayers II and III); and "the Virgin Mary, the Mother of God" (Prayer IV). Cardinal Newman's phrase, "The Glories of

Mary for the Sake of Her Son," is supremely applicable to the title "Mother of God," which was declared to be the faith of the Church at the Third Ecumenical Council, held at Ephesus, in 431 A.D. The Church's insistence on this title, Mother of God, is understandable, since no other formula makes so evident the intimate link between devotion to the Virgin Mary and belief in the Incarnation. This title was already in use in parts of the Church as early as the third century. The original form of the family prayer, "We fly to Thy patronage, O holy Mother of God" may also be that early.

The term "Mother of God" was used in Christian prayers before the doctrinal controversy that made it a test phrase of Christian faith. In 428 A.D. the term "Mother of God" was publicly challenged in Constantinople. The Church reacted strongly to this challenge at the Council of Ephesus. At stake was the central Christian truth that the man Jesus, Son of Mary, is truly "Son of God." Mary can be rightly called "Mother of God," not indeed in the blasphemous sense of having existed before God, but as in affirmation of the truth of the Incarnation. The Son of Mary is the one person Who is the Son of God, Emmanuel.

St. Cyril of Alexandria spoke for the Church's traditional faith when he wrote: "If we are to confess that Emmanuel is truly God, we must also confess that the Holy Virgin is *Theotokos* (Mother of God); for she bore according to the flesh the Word of God made flesh." St. Cyril's explanation of the term "Mother of God" shows that the center of attention must be Christ Himself: "Nor was He first born of the holy Virgin as an ordinary man, in such a way that the Word only afterwards descended upon Him; rather was He united with flesh in the womb itself, and thus is said to have undergone birth according to the flesh, inasmuch as He makes His own the birth of His own flesh. . . . For this reason the holy Fathers have boldly proclaimed the holy Virgin *Theotokos.*" Subsequent ecumenical councils, such as Chalcedon, 451 A.D., and II Constantinople, 553 A.D., made the meaning of "Mother of God" even more precise.

(Behold Your Mother, 62, 63, 64)*

PRAYER

MARY, Mother of God, I believe that the *most sublime of your privileges is your divine maternity.* Without that maternity, your other privileges would not exist; you yourself

---

* Note: BEHOLD YOUR MOTHER, Woman of Faith. A Pastoral Letter on the Blessed Virgin Mary. National Conference of Catholic Bishops, November 21, 1973.

would not exist, for you were created only to be the Mother of God.

Your divine maternity is great also because this privilege is the reason for your other privileges—your Immaculate Conception, miraculous virginity, fullness of grace, Assumption, and the spiritual maternity of all mankind.

I believe the teaching of the Church concerning the union of the human and divine natures in Christ: that Jesus Christ is God and man, perfect God and perfect man, and that this divinity and humanity are united in only one person so that the actions of the divine nature or the human nature are the actions of one person, the divine Person. Since God was born of you, you are the Mother of God. If we could not say that you are the Mother of God for having given a body to the Son of God, then we could neither adore this body; nor would we have been redeemed by the sacrifice of this body on the cross; nor would we be united to the divinity in receiving this body in the Eucharist.

Mary, *your divine maternity places you in a very wonderful relationship with the three divine Persons.* You are the loving *daughter of the Father,* because, before all creatures, you were predestined to be His daughter at the same moment that He decreed the Incarnation of His Son. He bestowed marvelous privileges upon you and loved you more than all other creatures together. As Mother of the Son of God, you are associated with the Father in the generation of His Son. With the Father you, too, can say, "This is My beloved Son in Whom I am well pleased."

You are the *Mother of the Son of God*. You fulfilled the duties and enjoy the rights of a true mother. From your own flesh and blood you formed the body of your Son. You nourished Him, clothed Him, educated Him. You commanded Him and He obeyed you. How can I ever understand the great love that bound your hearts together!

You are the *Bride of the Holy Spirit* because according to the Gospel and the teaching of the Apostles' Creed, you conceived of the Holy Spirit the Son of God, made man. You are called the temple of the Holy Spirit because, in virtue of your Immaculate Conception and your fullness of grace, He dwells within you in a most singular manner.

Mary, *your divine maternity is most cherished by you* because it is a token of God's special love for you. The divine motherhood permits you to love God with a very singular kind of love and to be loved by Him with an equally singular love. There is no closer bond of love among relationships than that which exists between a mother and her son. All your privileges increased your power to love God. Your Immaculate Conception permitted you to love God from the first instant of your existence; your virginity led you to vow an undivided love to Him; your fullness of grace made you capable of loving Him with the most intense love possible. No one could ever love God with the love of a mother. Only you could love God as your Son; only you could love your Son as God.

Mary, my Mother, the divine maternity itself, more than any particular privilege, is a mark of God's unequaled love for you. I rejoice with you in the happiness which fills your heart because of such love. I beg you to ask God that I return His love with some of the generosity and fervor with which you loved Him.

HYMN

O QUEEN of all the saints in heaven,
    Enthroned above the starry sky,
Who with your bosom's milk have fed,
Your own Creator, Lord most high.

What man had lost in mother Eve,
Your sacred womb to man restores;
To helpless children here on earth,
You opened heaven's eternal doors.

We greet you, Mother of God's Son!
O lead us to our Savior King.
Through you redeemed to endless life,
Your praise let all the nations sing!

O Jesus, born of Virgin fair,
Immortal glory be to You!
And praise to You, O Father, kind,
And Holy Spirit praise to You. Amen.

LITURGICAL PRAYERS

FATHER,
through the motherhood of the Virgin Mary,
You gave the human race eternal salvation.
May we feel the powerful help of her prayers in our lives,
for through her we received the very source of life,
Your Son, our Lord Jesus Christ,
Who lives and reigns with You and the Holy Spirit,
one God, forever. Amen.

Additional prayers: pp. 178, 191.

FEBRUARY

PRESENTATION OF THE LORD

February 2 (Novena: January 25)

DOCTRINE

IN REMEMBRANCE of the day on which God struck the first-born among the Egyptians and spared those of the Israelites, the Law of Moses ordained that every first-born son should be presented in the Temple of Jerusalem and should be redeemed by the payment of five shekels ($1.40). Also, every woman, after the birth of a male child, should offer for her legal purification a lamb and a turtledove. A poor woman might offer a second turtledove instead of the lamb. Accordingly, Mary and Joseph, taking the Child, went up to the Temple in Jerusalem and carried out the prescriptions of the Law. Mary's was entirely an external redeeming, for she knew well that she was buying Jesus back only to sacrifice Him more completely on the cross.

While in the Temple, they met a devout man named Simeon, to whom the Holy Spirit had revealed that he would not die before seeing the

Messiah. Prompted by the Holy Spirit, he recognized the long-awaited Savior in Jesus. Mary allowed him to take Jesus in his arms. As he did so, he exclaimed: "Now, Lord, You may dismiss Your servant in peace, according to Your word; for my eyes have seen Your salvation, which You have prepared in the sight of all the peoples, a light of revelation to the Gentiles and glory for Your people Israel" (Lk 2:29-32).

The prophecy brought home to the parents the fact that the mission of Jesus would extend to all nations and that this mission would entail suffering not only for the Savior but also for His Mother, for Simeon continued: "This Child is destined for the fall and rise of many in Israel, and to be a sign that will be opposed so that the secret thoughts of many will be revealed, and you yourself a sword will pierce" (Lk 2:34-35).

Mary has her Child in her arms again, but it is to offer Him in sacrifice. The Light of the World entered into His Temple at Jerusalem, and to celebrate this entry, the Church has prescribed a procession with lighted candles. The Temple was filled with glory and the Lord of Hosts gave His peace to the world when Mary carried her Son up the Temple steps at Jerusalem to present Him to the Lord.

We have evidence going back to the 5th century of the celebration at Jerusalem of the feast of the Presentation of the Lord in the Temple. Beginning with the 10th century Western liturgical books emphasized the purification of Mary. In full accord with the traditions of the Eastern Church it was established in 1960 that this must be regarded as a feast of the Lord, and yet it is one filled with the presence of His Mother.

Candles are blessed on this day, a symbolic representation of the words of Simeon concerning Christ: "A light of revelation to the Gentiles." A procession of the faithful with lighted candles is held to commemorate the entry of Christ, the Light of the World, into the Temple of Jerusalem. Mary's participation in the redeeming mission of her Son is expressed in the words of Simeon: "You yourself a sword will pierce."

THE CHURCH SPEAKS

THIS union of the Mother with the Son in the work of salvation is made manifest from the time of Christ's virginal conception up to His death. It is shown first of all when Mary, arising in haste to go to visit Elizabeth, was greeted by her as blessed because of her belief in the promise of salvation and the precursor leaped with joy in the womb of his mother. This union is manifest also at the birth of our Lord, who did not diminish His Mother's virginal integrity but sanctified it, when the Mother of God joyfully showed her firstborn Son to the shepherds and Magi.

When she presented Him to the Lord in the Temple, making the offering of the poor, she heard Simeon foretelling at the same time that her Son would be a sign of contradiction and that a sword would pierce the Mother's soul, that out of many hearts thoughts might be revealed. When the Child Jesus was lost and they had sought Him sorrowing, His parents found Him in the Temple, taken up with the things that were His Father's business; and they did not understand the word of their Son. His Mother indeed kept these things to be pondered over in her heart.

(Vatican II: *Constitution on the Church,* 57)

Since early times, but especially after the Council of Ephesus, devotion to Mary in the Church has grown wondrously. The People of God through the ages have shown her veneration and love. They have called upon her in prayer and they imitate her. All these ways of praising Mary draw us closer to Christ. When Mary is honored, her Son is duly acknowledged, loved and glorified, and His commandments are observed.

To venerate Mary correctly means to acknowledge her Son, for she is the Mother of God. To love her means to love Jesus, for she is always the Mother of Jesus. To pray to our Lady means not to substitute her for Christ, but to glorify her Son who desires us to have loving confidence in His Saints, especially in His Mother. To imitate the "faithful Virgin" means to keep her Son's commandments.

The better we come to know Mary of the Gospels as the Church views her in liturgical celebrations and popular commemorations, the more we will be led to imitate her. We may ask, however, how the two aspects of imitation and prayer are joined in devotion to Mary. Or, to put the question in another way: how are memory of the past and experiences of the present related in our devotion to the Mother of Jesus?

Through the Bible we recall what Mary once was in her earthly association with Jesus; but we also long to know what she means to us now, and why we pray to her. As Catholics, we believe that Mary was once joined to her Son's saving work on earth; but we also believe that she remains inseparably joined to Him, associated with the intercession the glorified Jesus makes for us forever at the throne of His Father (Heb 7:25).

(Behold Your Mother, 82, 83)

PRAYER

MARY, Mother of God, *I admire your obedience and humility in submitting to the law of purification* by presenting yourself in the Temple, like every other Jewish mother, forty days after the birth of Jesus. You were not bound by the Law, because you were a virgin as well as a mother. You hid your miraculous virginity under the mantle of humility. But the same spirit of humility which had induced Jesus to obey the law of circumcision made you also submit to the law of purification.

The God of holiness, having come upon the earth to take away the sins of the world, chose to appear among us as a sinner. It was, therefore, fitting that you, His immaculate Mother, destined to cooperate with Him in the work of Redemption, should teach the world, by your submission to the law of purification, this great truth, that humility is the beginning of our salvation, as pride has been the root of our ruin.

You were not obliged by the Law of Moses to present and ransom your first-born Son. In order to free yourself from legal uncleanness and to give us an example of obedience to God's Law, you submitted to the ceremony of the purification and made the offering demanded of the poor—two pigeons or turtledoves. In the fulfillment of the Law you gave an example of the most perfect obedience and zeal for the edification of others.

Mary, *the offering of Jesus was presented by your virginal hands.* Thus you associated yourself yet more directly and intimately with our salvation. You were the first to offer to the Eternal Father His Divine Son as the Victim for the world's Redemption. Here there was a sacrifice, and Jesus was the Victim. The victim had to belong to the person who offered it. But no child ever belonged to its mother as Jesus belonged to you. In this mystery Jesus is plainly a Victim, and also a Priest, but He could not better communicate His spirit of priesthood than by allowing you, His Mother, to present His outward offering. He could find no worthier altar on which to offer Himself than your immaculate hands. You really had the right to offer Jesus to His Heavenly Father in this mystery.

The Eternal Father once gave you the most precious treasure that heaven possessed—His own Divine Son. In the Temple, you returned to Him His gift by consecrating your Child to His honor and glory. For your generosity the Eternal Father made you, through Christ, the dispenser of the riches of God. In presenting your only Son, you present your all. For He was everything to you, and all else was nothing without Him.

Mary, *by your offering you sacrificed your own heart.* The holy old man Simeon took your Son in his arms. It was in your arms that he found the Savior, to remind us that he who desires to find Jesus will find Him through you. You heard Simeon's words as if they had been spoken to you by God Himself, "This Child is destined for the fall and rise of many in Israel, a sign that will be opposed so that the secret thoughts of many will be revealed, and you yourself a sword will pierce."

Since you were enlightened by the Scriptures, you realized that your Child would be opposed and utterly rejected by the Jews, who had, for forty centuries, unceasingly sighed for Him as a Savior. You knew that thousands even of His faithful followers throughout the world would turn from Him and would make His coming the occasion of their eternal ruin. You saw that from that moment you yourself would be pierced with a sword during the rest of your days.

I wish to offer myself as a sacrifice to God in union with Jesus and through your hands. Help me to sacrifice myself generously for the love of God—to abstain from those many hurtful things that prevent the union of my soul with God. In order to live, not to myself, but to God, I must bear the cross in union with Jesus. You suffered with Jesus and experienced in your soul what He underwent in His body. Let me never separate my sufferings from the sufferings of your Divine Son. May this loving union sustain me no matter how heavy my cross. He sends me the cross only to trace His image in my soul by uniting me closely with Himself. Let me realize that God, in His infinite wisdom, will make all things work together for my good.

HYMN

I WONDER, Lord, what words Your Mother said
  When You were cradled in her holy arms.
Her smile was love's caress upon Your head;
  Her eyes reflecting all Your baby charms.

Ah, never was there less of need to speak:
  The Word was there enthroned upon her knee.
What joy was left for either one to seek?
  For each shared in the other's destiny.

And both hearts beat in rhythm, each with each,
  Till something made her catch her breath and
    hold
You closer, something still beyond her reach—
  A sword would pierce her heart, she had been
    told.
You raised your lips to kiss away her fear,
  And saw within her shadowed eyes a tear.

LITURGICAL PRAYER

A LMIGHTY Father,
  Christ Your Son became man for us
and was presented in the Temple.
May He free our hearts from sin
and bring us into Your presence.
We ask this through our Lord Jesus Christ,
  Your Son,
Who lives and reigns with You and the Holy
  Spirit,
one God, forever. Amen.

Additional prayer: p. 186.

OUR LADY OF LOURDES

February 11 (Novena: February 2-10)

DOCTRINE

BETWEEN February 11 and July 16, 1858, the Blessed Virgin came down from heaven eighteen times and showed herself at Lourdes to Bernadette Soubirous, a little girl of fourteen years of age. On February 11, while gathering wood, Bernadette heard a whistle of wind. With astonished eyes she saw a niche in the upper part of a rock filled with golden light, and there in the midst of it stood a Lady of great beauty. Her robe glowed with the whiteness of snow in the sunshine and swept in majestic folds to the ground. Her head and shoulders were framed by a white veil, which fell the full length of her robe. A blue sash encircled her waist, and its two ends, wide and unornamented, reached down in front almost to her feet. Each of her feet bore a rose of purest gold. A rosary, whose beads were white and whose cross and chain were of gold, hung from her right arm. Her hands were open, and her arms outstretched slightly in front.

In her apparitions our Lady appealed for penance and prayers for sinners. On March 25, the day of the Annunciation, the Blessed Mother declared her name to Bernadette and to the world. On that day Bernadette made this request: "My Lady, would you be so kind as to tell me who you are?" This is how Bernadette describes what happened in that last apparition: "Three times I asked the Apparition her name. At the third instance, she stretched out her hands, which until then she had held joined, raised them, and she said: 'I am the Immaculate Conception.'" And having thus completed her great message to the world, the Lady smiled on Bernadette and withdrew without further word of farewell.

Less than four years before these apparitions, on December 8, 1854, Pope Pius IX proclaimed that Mary in the first instant of her conception was preserved free from all stain of original sin through the merits of her Divine Son. At Lourdes the Virgin Mary had come to confirm the infallible utterance of God's Vicar on earth and declared herself not only immaculately conceived, but "the Immaculate Conception." Mary's purpose in appearing to Bernadette, who later became a saint, was to warn the child to pray and make sacrifices for sinners. The many miracles performed at Lourdes are the proof that this message was an authentic warning from the Queen of the Universe to her children and that she is deeply interested in their welfare.

THE CHURCH SPEAKS

IN THE interim just as the Mother of Jesus, glorified in body and soul in heaven, is the image and beginning of the Church as it is to be perfected in the world to come, so too does she shine forth on earth, until the day of the Lord shall come, as a sign of sure hope and solace to the People of God during its sojourn on earth. . . .

The entire body of the faithful pours forth instant supplications to the Mother of God and Mother of men that she, who aided the beginnings of the Church by her prayers, may now, exalted as she is above all the angels and saints, intercede before her Son in the fellowship of all the saints, until all families of people, whether they are honored with the title of Christian or whether they still do not know the Savior, may be happily gathered together in peace and harmony into one People of God, for the glory of the Most Holy and Undivided Trinity.

(Vatican II: *Constitution on the Church*, 68, 69)

We turn our reflections now to the authenticated appearances of our Lady and their influence on Catholic devotion especially in the years since the Apparition at Lourdes, in 1858. Other 19th century events of this kind were the experiences of St. Catherine Labouré in 1830 (the "Miraculous Medal"), and the apparition at La Salette in 1846. In our own hemisphere we recall the apparition in 1531 of Our Lady of Guadalupe, "Queen of the Americas." Best known of the 20th century appearances of the Mother of the Lord is that at Fatima, in 1917.

These providential happenings serve as reminders to us of basic Christian themes: prayer, penance, and the necessity of the sacraments. After due investigation, the Church has approved the pilgrimages and other devotions associated with certain private revelations. She has also at times certified the holiness of their recipients by beatification and canonization, for example, St. Bernadette of Lourdes and St. Catherine Labouré. The Church judges the devotions that have sprung from these extraordinary events in terms of its own traditional standards. Catholics are encouraged to practice such devotions when they are in conformity with authentic devotion to Mary.

Even when a "private revelation" has spread to the entire world, as in the case of Our Lady of Lourdes, and has been recognized in the liturgical calendar, the Church does not make mandatory the acceptance either of the original story or of particular forms of piety springing from it. With the Vatican Council we remind true lovers of our Lady of the danger of superficial sentiment and vain credulity. Our faith does not seek new gospels, but leads us to know the excellence of the Mother of God and moves us to a filial love toward our Mother and to the imitation of her virtues.

(Behold Your Mother, 99, 100)

PRAYER

MARY Mother of God, *God spoke of you as the Woman who would crush the serpent's head.* Faith tells us that the fall of man was the effect of the malice and envy of the devil, who sought in this way to be revenged upon the Creator for having cast him out of paradise in punishment for his rebellion. But God turned the scheme of the evil one back upon its inventor. A man and a woman had both taken part in the degradation of our race; they must both have part in its restoration. Jesus is the new Adam and you are the new Eve.

The Lord God said to the serpent, "Because you have done this, you will be the most cursed of all the animals and of all the wild beasts. . . . I will establish hostility between you and the woman, and between your line and her line. Her offspring will crush your head and you will bruise his heal" (Gen 3:14-15).

As the Immaculate Conception, you are the Woman who appeared as the mortal enemy of the serpent. Your Divine Son was destined to

crush the serpent's head by releasing mankind
from slavery of Satan, thus putting an end to
the empire of sin. When God pronounced
doom against the evil one, He also announced
His merciful plan of saving mankind from the
effects of the guilt of our first parents. This was
the earliest promise of a Redeemer to come,
and you were to be His immaculate Mother.

Mary, the beloved disciple, St. John, tells us
that "a great sign appeared in heaven, a
woman clothed with the sun, with the moon
beneath her feet, and a crown of twelve stars on
her head" (Rev 12:1). The Woman is a striking
image of you, the Immaculate Conception.
The attitude of the Church toward you, symbolized by the moon under your feet, is that of
a suppliant who is forever entreating you to use
your power in favor of your children. She is forever imploring you to intercede in their behalf
with Him Who has clothed you with His light
and His glory, and has poured out upon you
the fullness of His grace.

Mary, *I firmly believe in the doctrine of Holy
Mother Church concerning your Immaculate
Conception*; namely, that you were, in the first
instant of your conception, by the singular
grace and privileges of God, in view of the merits of Jesus Christ, the Savior of the human
race, preserved immune from all stain of original sin.

It was fitting that the God of all purity spring from the greatest purity. Alone of all the children of Adam, you were gifted with the fullness of sanctifying grace which made you the object of a very special love on the part of God. How wonderful were the workings of divine power to make you a fitting dwelling for the Redeemer of the world! With no tendency to evil, but with a deep yearning for the highest virtue, you glorified God more than all His other creatures. At the very instant of your conception your mind was filled with the light of God, and your will was entirely conformed to the Divine Will. You were always intimately united with God.

Help me to imitate your holiness to some degree. Your holiness was not the result of the privilege of your Immaculate Conception and sanctifying grace alone, but followed from your gift of yourself to God and your constant cooperation with His graces. Help me to be generous with God by turning to good account the graces that He ever bestows on me, and by rising promptly when I fall, with renewed confidence in His mercy. Aid me through your prayers with your Divine Son, to be a true child of yours, as Bernadette was, and to grow daily into your likeness.

LITURGICAL PRAYER

GOD of infinite mercy,
we celebrate the feast of Mary,
Our Lady of Lourdes,
the sinless Mother of God.
May her prayers help us to rise above our
human weakness.
We ask this through our Lord Jesus Christ,
Your Son,
Who lives and reigns with You and the Holy
Spirit,
one God, forever. Amen.

Additional prayer: p. 192.

MARCH

ANNUNCIATION OF OUR LORD

March 25 (Novena: March 16-24)

DOCTRINE

ABOUT the time of the espousals of Mary and Joseph, the angel Gabriel was sent to Mary at Nazareth and greeted her: "Hail, full of grace! The Lord is with you" (Lk 1:28). Mary was disturbed by this greeting and wondered what it could mean, but the angel reassured her that she had found grace before God; that is, she was the object of a very special privilege in His eyes. "You will conceive in your womb and bear a son, and you will name Him Jesus. He will be great and will be called Son of the Most High." The angel clearly foretold the Messiah Who had been yearned for during centuries by all pious Jews. Now Mary was invited to become His Mother.

She asked how this could happen since she had resolved to remain a virgin. The angel told her that

He Who would be born of her was the Son of God, and that is why He would be born of her virginity, by a miracle of God. She would have only to consent to the action of the Holy Spirit Who would work the miracle of the Incarnation in her womb. "The Holy Spirit will come upon you, and the power of the Most High will overshadow you. Therefore, the child to be born will be holy, and He will be called the Son of God." Then, to give further proof, he told of the conception of John, likewise contrary to the ordinary laws of nature.

This was the most solemn instant in the history of mankind. The salvation or the loss of innumerable souls depended on her answer. And Mary said calmly, "I am the servant of the Lord. Let it be done to me according to your word." At that moment, as St. John states: "The Word became flesh and dwelt among us. And we saw His glory, the glory as of the Father's only Son, full of grace and truth" (Jn 1:14).

The Solemnity of the Annunciation, of Eastern origin, was accepted at Rome in the 7th century under the title "Annunciation of the Lord," to make it more evident that it is above all a feast of the Lord. This feast recalls the greatest event in history, the Incarnation of our Lord in the womb of a Virgin. On this day the Word was made flesh, and united to Himself forever the humanity of Jesus. This feast is the anniversary of the ordination of Christ as a Priest, for it is by anointing of the Divinity that He has become Supreme Pontiff, Mediator between God and man.

The mystery of the Incarnation has earned for Mary her most glorious title, that of "Mother of God." Since the title of Mother of God makes Mary all-powerful with her Son, we should have recourse to her intercession with Him for the sanctification and salvation of our souls.

THE CHURCH SPEAKS

THE Father of mercies willed that the Incarnation should be preceded by the acceptance of her who was predestined to be the Mother of His Son, so that just as a woman contributed to death, so also a woman should contribute to life. That is true in outstanding fashion of the Mother of Jesus, who gave to the world Him Who is Life itself and Who renews all things, and Who was enriched by God with the gifts which befit such a role. It is no wonder therefore that the usage prevailed among the Fathers whereby they called the Mother of God entirely holy and free from all stain of sin, as though fashioned by the Holy Spirit and formed as a new creature.

Adorned from the first instant of her conception with the radiance of an entirely unique holiness, the Virgin of Nazareth is greeted, on God's command, by an angel messenger as "full of grace," and to the heavenly messenger she replies: "Behold the handmaid of the Lord; be it done unto me according to your word" (Lk 1:38). Thus Mary, a daughter of

Adam, consenting to the divine Word, became the Mother of Jesus, the one and only Mediator. Embracing God's salvific will with a full heart and impeded by no sin, she devoted herself totally as a handmaid of the Lord to the person and work of her Son, under Him and with Him, by the grace of almighty God, serving the mystery of redemption.

Rightly therefore the holy Fathers see her as used by God not merely in a passive way, but as freely cooperating in the work of human salvation through faith and obedience. For, as St. Irenaeus says, she, "being obedient, became the cause of salvation for herself and for the whole human race." Hence not a few of the early Fathers gladly assert in their preaching: "The knot of Eve's disobedience was untied by Mary's obedience; what the virgin Eve bound through her unbelief, the Virgin Mary loosened by her faith." Comparing Mary with Eve, they call her "the Mother of the living," and still more often they say: "death through Eve, life through Mary."

(Vatican II: *Constitution on the Church*, 56)

In St. Luke's beautiful, balanced story, our Lady's words come next: "How can this be, since I do not know man?" Mary's question is evidence of the belief of the early Church that Jesus was virginally conceived, the doctrine usually called the "Virgin Birth." Gabriel's reply to Mary's question leads into the second main part of his message: that the holy Child to be born of Mary will be not only the promised Messiah, but God made man.

The angel explains the virginal conception of Jesus as being due to the power of God Who has chosen this unique way to send His Son among men as their true brother and Savior. In Jesus, mankind gets a fresh start. The conception of the Son of Mary without a human father is the sign that the Incarnation is the new creation, independent of the will of man or urge of the flesh (Jn 1:13). The merciful Father intervenes in human history to send the new Adam, born of the Virgin Mary through the power of the Spirit.

"Hence, the offspring to be born will be called Son of God" (Lk 1:35). The title "Son of God" provides solid ground for us to profess our faith in the divinity of Jesus. Yet Gabriel's words offer an even more subtle and profound reason for affirming that the Son of Mary is truly the Son of God, Emmanuel, God-with us. . . .

The ark of the covenant and the covering cloud influence St. Luke's narrative. In his account, however, the vivifying power of the unseen Spirit overshadows the Virgin, and God is made visibly present as the Son of Mary. The Mother of Jesus is the new and perfect ark of the covenant, the living tabernacle

of the divine presence. The sacred ark that dis-
appeared six centuries before has now returned
in a more perfect way. Mary is the living ark of
the covenant carrying Jesus. Salvation comes
through Mary's flesh, through Mary's faith. . . .

The episode of the Annunciation concludes
with a double tribute to Mary's faith. The bet-
ter-known is Mary's word of consent; her
maternal "yes" was also her act of faith: "I am
the servant of the Lord. Let it be done to me as
you say" (Lk 1:38). These words have echoed
and re-echoed in Christian liturgy and litera-
ture from earliest times. The chapter on Mary
in the *Dogmatic Constitution on the Church*
may be regarded as an extended commentary
on her consent at the Annunciation. The
opening sentence of number 53 is typical: "At
the message of the angel, the Virgin Mary
received the Word of God into her heart and
her body, and gave Life to the world."

(Behold Your Mother, 24, 25, 28)

PRAYER

MARY, Mother of God, *how great was the
honor given to you* at the Annunciation!
Within your humble home in the little town of
Nazareth, the Holy Spirit willed to perform a
miracle that was the masterpiece of infinite
power—the Incarnation of the Son of God.
God sent Gabriel, one of His glorious archangels, to deliver the most important message

in the history of mankind, announcing the coming of the Savior of the world and the selection of you to be His Mother. Thus was fulfilled the prophecy that Christ would be born of the family of David.

With heavenly homage the angelic messenger greeted you: "Hail, full of grace! The Lord is with you. Blessed are you among women" (Lk 1:28). Never before did angel greet man with such words. In all humility you attributed this holiness to God, working wondrously within you. When the Triune God destined and elevated you, a mortal Virgin, to the dignity of the Mother of the Redeemer, the *Father* had to endow you with a fullness of perfection suitable for such a dignity. *The Son*, the Eternal Wisdom of God, in choosing you for His Mother, bestowed on you a certain fullness of grace, so that as you gave Christ His human nature, Christ, in a certain sense, raised you as close to God as a mere creature can come. And the *Holy Spirit*, Who descended upon you in the Incarnation with all His fullness, must have conferred upon you such treasures of sanctity as would prepare you to receive the Son of God in your most pure womb.

"The Lord is with you." He was with you in a manner more intimate, more perfect, and more divine that He ever was or will be with any other creature. He was with you not only by His essence, His presence, and His power, as He is with all His creatures. He was with you not only with His actual grace, touching your heart and enlightening your understanding. He was with you not only by His sanctifying grace, making you pleasing in His sight, as He is present with all the just. He was with you not only by a special protection guiding you in His ways and leading you securely to salvation. He was with you, and with you alone, in an unspeakable manner by bodily presence. In you, and of your substance, was this day formed His adorable body. In you He reposed for nine months, with His whole Divinity and humanity.

The angel said to you, "Blessed are you among women." Your blessedness was due to your unexcelled sanctity. You would be hailed by all generations as blessed above all other women because you are the Mother of God and at the same time a spotless Virgin. You are blessed because of the fullness of grace you received; blessed because of the greatness of the mercy to be bestowed on you; blessed because of the Majesty of the Person Who was to take flesh of you; blessed because of the glory which would become yours.

Mary, the instant that you gave your consent to the archangel, *the Holy Spirit overshadowed you and wrought in your most chaste womb the Incarnation of the Son of God.* How consistent with the infinite tenderness of God that His Christ, the Immortal Child, should be conceived by the power of the Holy Spirit in the body of a young virgin and that a virgin should bear a Child to redeem the world! In that moment the mystery of love and mercy, promised to mankind thousands of years earlier, foretold by so many prophets, desired by so many saints, was accomplished upon earth.

In that instant the Word of God became forever united to humanity; the human soul of Jesus Christ, produced from nothing, began to enjoy God and to know all things past, present, and to come. From your pure blood the Holy Spirit formed the pure body of Jesus. At that moment God began to have an Adorer Who was infinite, and the world a Mediator Who was all-powerful. In the working of this great mystery you also were chosen to cooperate by your free consent.

Mary, not only were you full of grace, but you also bore the Author of grace. You were entirely under the influence of Christ's divinity. In return for the natural strength that you gave Him, He gave you His divine strength. You were united with Him as closely as a mother is united with her child. Your heart beat in unison with His heart.

I rejoice with you that you are so privileged, so exalted as to become the worthy Mother of

God. We all rejoice because all the graces and spiritual benefits we have received and shall receive, all future glory comes from this exalted mystery of the Incarnation. I thank God for the great glory he has bestowed upon you for which all generations shall call you blessed. I thank you for the motherly compassion with which you came to the aid of a helpless race by consenting to be the Mother of our Savior.

HYMN

HAIL, bright Star of ocean,
     God's own Mother blest,
Ever-sinless Virgin,
Gate of heavenly rest!

Taking that sweet Ave
Which from Gabriel came,
Peace confirm within us,
Changing Eva's name.

Break the captive's fetters,
Light on blindness pour:
All our ills expelling,
Every bliss implore.

Show thyself a Mother;
May the Word Divine,
     Born for us thine Infant,
Hear our prayers through thine.

Virgin all excelling,
Mildest of the mild,
Freed from guilt, preserve us
Meek and undefiled.

Keep our life all spotless,
Make our way secure,
Till we find in Jesus
Joy forevermore.

Through the highest heaven
To the Almighty Three,
Father, Son and Spirit,
One same glory be. Amen.

LITURGICAL PRAYER

ALMIGHTY Father of our Lord Jesus
Christ,
You have made known the beauty of Your
power
by exalting the humble virgin of Nazareth
and making her the Mother of our Savior.
May her prayers bring Jesus to the waiting
world
and fill its void with the presence of her Child,
Who lives and reigns with You and the Holy
Spirit,
one God, forever. Amen.

Additional prayers: pp. 178, 184, 191.

MAY

VISITATION

May 31 (Novena: May 22-30)

DOCTRINE

THE archangel Gabriel revealed to Mary the miraculous motherhood of her cousin Elizabeth and invited her to visit her home. Love urged her to make this visit at once to the hill country to a town of Judea. Christ, Whom she was now carrying, prompted her to begin her mission of bringing Him to souls. The trip must have lasted about four days, for the village to which she was going was located a few miles beyond Jerusalem.

Mary remained with her relatives about three months, till John the Baptist was born. They were months of great happiness for her and of blessings for Elizabeth and her son. The aged priest Zechariah suddenly recovered his power of speech, which he had lost because he did not believe the angel in the Temple who announced that his wife would give him a son who would prepare the way for the Messiah. In the inspired canticle he began to praise God for having come to redeem His people.

The feast of the Visitation commemorates Mary's visit to her cousin Elizabeth, the sanctification of John the Baptist in his mother's womb, and the occasion on which the Blessed Virgin uttered her hymn of thanksgiving, the Magnificat. The feast was instituted in 1389 by Urban VI to obtain the end of the Western schism.

In this mystery of our Lady's life God wished to show us that Mary is the instrument and means by which He imparts to us His graces. She is truly interested in our sanctification and salvation.

We should admire the consideration Mary showed for Elizabeth. Our heavenly Mother is our model in carrying out the second great commandment of love. Through her intercession we should ask Jesus for the graces we need, especially that of being kind to our neighbor.

THE CHURCH SPEAKS

THE Sacred Scriptures, of both the Old and New Testament, as well as ancient Tradition show the role of the Mother of the Savior in the economy of salvation in an ever clearer light and draw attention to it. The books of the Old Testament describe the history of salvation, by which the coming of Christ into the world was slowly prepared. These earliest documents, as they are read in the Church and are understood in the light of a further and full revelation, bring the figure of the woman, Mother of the Redeemer, into a gradually clearer light.

When it is looked at in this way, she is already prophetically foreshadowed in the promise of victory over the serpent which was given to our first parents after their fall into sin. Likewise she is the Virgin who shall conceive and bear a Son, Whose name will be called Emmanuel. She stands out among the poor and humble of the Lord, who confidently hope for and receive salvation from Him. With her the exalted Daughter of Zion, and after a long expectation of the promise, the times are fulfilled and the new economy established, when the Son of God took a human nature from her, that He might in the mysteries of His flesh free man from sin.

(Vatican II: *Constitution on the Church*, 55)

Luke begins his Gospel by taking us into the company of poor and holy people: Elizabeth and Zechariah, Anna and Simeon, Joseph and Mary. Jesus Himself and the Good News came from this circle, cradle of the Christian Church. For St. Luke, Mary is the perfect example of awaiting the Messiah with a pure and humble spirit. Luke sees in Mary the Daughter of Zion who rejoices because God is with her, and who praises His greatness for pulling down the mighty and exalting the humble. . . .

The "ark of the covenant" theme continues in St. Luke's account of Mary's visit to her cousin, Elizabeth. The Old Testament counterpart is provided by the story of the transfer of the ark of the covenant by King David (2 Sm 6). . . . "The ark of the Lord remained in the house of Obed-edom the Gittite for three months, and the Lord blessed Obed-edom and his whole house."—As St. Luke tells it, Mary remained "about three months" and clearly Zechariah's whole house received great blessing from the presence of Mary's unborn Son. . . .

Gabriel concludes his message with the unexpected news of Elizabeth's pregnancy, and then repeats the powerful words associated with Abraham in Genesis: "for nothing is impossible with God" (Lk 1:37). St. Luke places Mary, daughter of Abraham, before us as the great Gospel model of faith. He applies to her virginal motherhood the promise made to Abraham, remote ancestor of the Messiah. In the strength of her faith, Mary consents to the merciful Father's invitation, and in the power of the Spirit becomes the Mother of Jesus, Son of God in human flesh.

(*Behold Your Mother,* 17, 24, 27, 33)

PRAYER

MARY, Mother of God, *your love is strikingly shown forth in the Visitation.* When you learned from the angel that your cousin Elizabeth was with child and needed your help, you set out to care for her. Neither your long absence from home, nor the inconvenience of a difficult and dangerous journey to the mountain country, kept you from making this mission of love. You thought only of the good you could do in Elizabeth's home. Your sincere love made you hasten to be of service. As you entered the house of Zechariah and greeted your aged cousin, you offered kind words of comfort and congratulation. You lovingly served her till you saw her happily delivered of the child of promise with which God has blessed her.

How humble you were! Though you were the Mother of the Most High, you wanted to become the nurse of Elizabeth and the infant John. Though declared blessed among women, you considered yourself the servant of two of God's beloved children.

Help me to strive to imitate your wonderful charity by aiding those who are in need, by sympathizing with those who are afflicted, by opening my heart and applying my hands to relieve every form of distress. Give me love like yours, which recognized in every human being a brother or sister in Jesus Christ, to be treated with respect and tenderness and to be aided according to the measure of my power. Teach me that the test of my following of your Divine Son is practical charity. Help me, above all, so

that by my good example I may enrich and
ennoble every human being whose life I touch.

May the thought of your tenderness and love
increase my confidence in you and make me
look up to you in all the dangers that surround
me in life. I am sure that you, who are all-powerful as my advocate, will not desert me but will
bring to my poor soul grace and sanctification.

Mary, *the results of your visit to Elizabeth
were wonderful.* Scarcely had you greeted your
aged cousin, when mother and son felt at once
the sanctifying effects of your loving presence.
The child in the womb of Elizabeth was sanctified and exulted for joy at the presence of Jesus.
At the sound of your voice Elizabeth was filled
with the Holy Spirit and began to prophesy:
"Blessed are you among women, and blessed is
the fruit of your womb." She humbly exclaimed, "And why am I so favored that the
mother of my Lord should visit me?" God
freed His future messenger from original sin
and enriched him with grace. Elizabeth proclaimed that you were the Mother of Christ
and declared you blessed among women
because you were the most holy dwelling of the
Eternal God.

The effects of the presence of Jesus and you
are still the same. Grace comes to us from Jesus
and reaches us through you. Elizabeth received
the Holy Spirit through your intervention, in

order to teach us that we must make use of you as our Mediatrix with your Divine Son, if we wish to obtain the Holy Spirit. It is true that we could go directly to God and ask Him for His grace without your help, but God has not willed it so.

In the mystery of the Visitation you began your office of bringing Jesus into the souls of men. With joy you must have foreseen the millions of souls who by your presence in their lives would cast off the bonds of sin. Through this mystery enlighten my mind with divine truth; warm my heart with heavenly love; strengthen me to win the victory over my evil inclinations and the power of evil.

Mary, *how beautifully you expressed your gratitude and humility!* Unmindful of your dignity and greatness, you thought only of returning thanks to God, to Whom you attributed all your greatness and privileges. God has exalted you above all creatures. You thought only of praising Him as your greatest Benefactor when you exclaimed, "My soul proclaims the greatness of the Lord and my spirit rejoices in God my Savior. . . . The Mighty One has done great things for me."

In your humility you looked upon yourself as His lowly servant. Though you prophesied that all generations would call you blessed, you attributed all holiness to God. The glory of the great things that had been done in you, you attributed to God's mercy and power and love. God has raised you to the highest dignity in His power in choosing you to be the Mother of His Son. The whole human race rejoices in you as Queen and Mother.

Teach me ever to seek the glory of God and to render to Him what is His divine right. God looks for gratitude and humility which draw down upon us His favor and His gifts. God wants His gifts recognized. Help me to return unceasing thanks to God for His many favors, and keep me humble in possessing and using them. May I be found worthy of your frequent visits with Jesus to my heart in this life and of the invitation to come and live with you both for all eternity in heaven.

MARY'S CANTICLE

MY SOUL proclaims the greatness of the Lord and my spirit rejoices in God my Savior.
For He has looked with favor on the lowliness of His servant;
    henceforth all generations will call me blessed.
The Mighty One has done great things for me,
    and holy is His Name.
His mercy is shown from age to age
    to those who fear Him.
He has shown the strength of His arm,
    He has routed those who are arrogant in the desires of their hearts.
He has brought down the mighty from their thrones
    and lifted up the lowly.

He has filled the hungry with good things
  and sent the rich away empty.
He has come to the aid of Israel His servant,
  ever mindful of His merciful love,
according to the promises He made to our ancestors,
  to Abraham and to his descendants forever.

(Lk 1:46-55)

LITURGICAL PRAYER

ETERNAL Father,
  You inspired the Virgin Mary, Mother of
  Your Son,
to visit Elizabeth and help in her need.
Open our hearts to the working of Your Spirit,
and with Mary may we praise You forever.
We ask this through our Lord Jesus Christ,
  Your Son,
Who lives and reigns with You and the Holy
  Spirit,
one God, forever. Amen.

Additional prayers: 175, 178, 193.

IMMACULATE HEART OF MARY

Saturday following the Second Sunday after Pentecost
(Novena: Thursday before the Second Sunday)

DOCTRINE

THE object of the devotion to the Immaculate Heart of Mary is to love Jesus better by uniting ourselves to Mary and by imitating her virtues. Her Immaculate Heart is the model of virtue and sanctity.

The great love and care that the Immaculate Heart of Mary has for all of us was shown by her apparitions at Fatima, Portugal, from May to October of 1917. Six times did she deign to appear to the three shepherd children—Lucia, Jacinta, and Francesco—to convey to them her great concern for the spiritual welfare of mankind and to request that ungrateful mankind stop offending Jesus. The means she suggested were reparation to her Immaculate Heart through the daily Rosary and the devotion of the first Saturdays.

Our Lady stated that her Heart is the hope of the world. She expressly requested the practice and spread of devotion to her Immaculate Heart, saying that it is in the designs of the Divine Mercy to help the world through this Heart. "To save souls God wishes to establish in the world the devotion to my Immaculate Heart. If they do what I will tell you, many souls will be saved, and there will be peace. I come to ask the consecration of Russia to my Immaculate Heart and the Communion of Reparation of the (five) first Saturdays. If they listen to my requests, Russia will be converted and there will be peace. . . . In the end my Immaculate Heart will triumph."

In May of 1943, Pope Pius XII urged Catholics to invoke the intercession of the Blessed Virgin, especially by reciting the Rosary, for the needs of humanity and the attainment of a just peace, and asked them to consecrate themselves to her Immaculate Heart. The object of the Feast of the Immaculate Heart of Mary, instituted by Pope Pius XII in 1945, is to promote devotion to the Immaculate Heart of Mary so that through her intercession all nations may enjoy peace and religious liberty, sinners may be converted and all the faithful may advance in virtue.

THE CHURCH SPEAKS

WHILE in the most holy Virgin the Church has already reached that perfection whereby she is without spot or wrinkle, the followers of Christ still strive to increase in holiness by conquering sin. And so they turn their eyes to Mary who shines forth to the whole community of the elect as the model of

virtues. Piously meditating on her and contemplating her in the light of the Word made
man, the Church with reverence enters more
intimately into the great mystery of the
Incarnation and becomes more and more like
her Spouse.

For Mary, who since her entry into salvation
history unites in herself and reechoes the greatest teachings of the faith as she is proclaimed
and venerated, calls the faithful to her Son and
His sacrifice and to the love of the Father.
Seeking after the glory of Christ, the Church
becomes more like her exalted Type, and continually progresses in faith, hope and charity,
seeking and doing the will of God in all things.

(Vatican II: *Constitution on the Church*, 65)

It is a cherished American Catholic custom
to call the Mother of Jesus "our Blessed
Mother." In many respects this title can be
explained in the same way as "Mediatrix."
Still, it has its own special value. "Mother"
belongs to the transmission of life. The reference here is to our life in Christ. St. Paul's
familiar comparison likens the Church to a
human body with Christ as Head, and the
faithful as its members. Like the Savior's para-
ble of the vine and branches, the image of the
Church as "body of Christ" is a graphic
reminder that the same life links members to
Head, branches to Vine.

From earliest Christian times the Church was regarded as "Mother Church." Gradually, Mary's relationship to the sons and daughters of the Church came to be regarded also as that of "spiritual mother." Physically Mother of Christ the Head, Mary is spiritually Mother of the members of Christ. She is Mother of all men, for Christ died for all. She is especially the Mother of the faithful, or as Pope Paul proclaimed during the Second Vatican Council, she is "Mother of the Church."

It is important to understand what is meant by the title, "our Blessed Mother." Mary is not spiritual Mother of men solely because she was physical Mother of the Savior. Nonetheless, the full understanding of Mary's motherhood of Jesus contains also the secret of her spiritual motherhood of the brethren of Christ. This secret is the truth already given in the Gospels and constantly stressed ever since in Christian thought and piety: Mary consented in faith to become the Mother of Jesus.

The Second Vatican Council was in the stream of the constant tradition of the Church when it said that Mary received the Word of God into her heart and her body at the angel's announcement and thereby brought Life to the world. She conceived in her heart, with her whole being, before she conceived in her womb. First came Mary's faith, then her motherhood. Faith is the key also to the spiritual motherhood of Mary. By her faith she became the perfect example of what the Gospels mean by "spiritual motherhood." In the preaching of the Savior, His "mother" is whoever hears God's word and keeps it. All who truly follow Christ become "mother" of Christ, for by their faith they bring Him to birth in others.

(Behold Your Mother, 71, 72)

PRAYER

MARY, Mother of God, your heart is *a shrine of holiness* in which the demon of sin has never entered; whose sanctuary was never once defiled by the least touch of evil; whose altar was the chosen resting place of the Holy Spirit. After the Sacred Heart of Jesus, never was there a heart more pure and more holy.

The Eternal Father takes pleasure in looking upon your heart as the masterpiece of His divine power. The Son takes pleasure in it as the heart of His Mother, the source from which He drew the blood that ransomed us. The Holy Spirit dwells in you as in a temple.

Your heart is *a shrine of peace*, for it is the heart of the Mother of the Prince of Peace, a heart never for a moment disturbed by evil passion, a heart whose gifts to mankind are mercy, love, and peace. To all of us your immaculate heart after that of Jesus is most loving and most merciful. How many afflicted hearts are consoled in you! How many frail hearts are strengthened by you! How many are now in heaven because of the protection given them by your merciful heart! We obtain everything for our peace of soul in time and eternity from the Father through the Heart of Jesus and everything from Jesus through your heart. You are truly the "Queen of Peace."

Your heart is *a shrine adorned with all the skill of the Divine Creator,* Who has lavished upon it the riches of His treasure house — sanctifying grace, greater in worth than all the riches of the world.

Your heart is *the masterpiece of the Holy Trinity.* The Eternal Father unfolded His omnipotence in order to form in you a heart full of sweetness and obedience to your Creator. The Divine Son gave you a mother's heart, in which, as in a sanctuary, He wished to dwell. The Holy Spirit gave you the heart of a bride, all burning with a love pure and ardent. Your heart is truly a mirror of all the virtues, a vivid image and faithful copy of the Sacred Heart of Jesus.

Mary, your heart is *a counterpart of the Heart of Jesus.* His Heart is a loving Heart, and that love is symbolized by the flames which St. Margaret Mary saw coming forth from it. Your heart is also the most affectionate of hearts after that of Jesus. You love us as a mother loves her children. Your eyes ever watch over us; your ears ever listen to our cries; your hands are ever extended over us to help us and impart heavenly gifts to us; above all, your heart is full of tenderest care for us.

But your love for God was even greater. God inflamed no other heart, after that of the Heart of His Son, with His love so much as yours. Free from all attachment to earthly things, you were most capable of being filled with divine love. Such love set your heart on fire with love for your Divine Son, not only as your Son, but also as your God and Savior, since you had shared in advance in the merits of His Passion and death.

The Heart of Jesus was a *suffering* Heart, symbolized by the thorns encircling it, the cross above it, and the gash opened in its side. Your heart was also a suffering heart. Its martyrdom began with Simeon's prophecy in the Temple and was completed on Calvary. When the hands and feet of Jesus were pierced with nails, the sound of each blow of the hammer inflicted a wound in your heart. When His side was opened with a lance, a sword of anguish also pierced your heart.

The Heart of Jesus was a *pure* Heart. Your heart was also a pure heart, free from the stain of original sin, from the least stain of actual sin. Your heart is pure and spotless because sanctified beyond all other hearts by the indwelling of the Holy Spirit, making it worthy to be the dwelling place of the Sacred Heart of Jesus. Hence the Church pays loving respect to your Immaculate Heart.

The Heart of Jesus was a *generous* Heart, symbolized by the wound in His side from which came forth the last drops of His Heart's Blood shed for us, and by which we can reach the treasures of that Divine Heart. Your heart is also a generous heart, full of love, abounding in mercy. All mankind may find a place there as your children, if they only choose to listen to your loving appeal. Your heart is a refuge for sinners, for you are the Mother of Mercy, who has never been known to turn away anyone who came to seek your aid.

Mary, your Immaculate Heart is *the Hope of the world*. In your apparitions at Fatima you revealed that it is the design of the Divine Mercy to cure the world through your heart. As the heart of a mother triumphs over the just anger of a father in an earthly family, so your heart will triumph by averting the force of God's justice upon this sinful world. In your six apparitions at Fatima you made repeated demands for penance and reparation.

Grant that we all may heed your warning, for only through penance and reparation can we blot out sin and the insult it inflicts on God.

Be pleased to lead mankind securely to certain victory over Communism through the triumph of your Immaculate Heart as you promised at Fatima: "In the end my Immaculate Heart will triumph and an era of peace will be conceded to mankind."

I consecrate myself entirely to your Immaculate Heart. I consecrate to you my very being and my whole life: all that I have, all that I love, all that I am. I desire that all that is in me and around me may belong to you and may share in the benefits of your motherly blessing.

LITURGICAL PRAYER

FATHER,
You prepared the heart of the Virgin Mary
to be a fitting dwelling place for Your Holy
   Spirit.
By her prayers for us
may our soul become a more worthy temple of
   Your glory.
Grant this through our Lord Jesus Christ, Your
   Son,
Who lives and reigns with You and the Holy
   Spirit,
one God, forever. Amen.

Additional prayer: p. 196.

JULY

OUR LADY OF MOUNT CARMEL

July 16 (Novena: July 7-15)

DOCTRINE

A CCORDING to tradition, a number of men who embraced the Christian faith on Pentecost Day erected a church to the Blessed Mary of Mount Carmel. These religious came to Europe in the 13th century, when Mary is said to have appeared to their General, Simon Stock, at Cambridge, England, on July 16, 1251. In answer to his appeal for help for his oppressed order, she appeared to him with a scapular in her hand and said, "Take this scapular of your order as a badge of my confraternity and for you and all Carmelites a special sign of grace; whoever dies in this garment, will not suffer everlasting fire. It is the sign of salvation, a safeguard in dangers, a pledge of peace and of the covenant." Indirectly the promise is extended to all who are devoted to the Mother of God.

The Scapular devotion is one of the oldest devotions to our Lady. It has been widespread in the Church for nearly seven centuries and is blessed with many indulgences. The Scapular of Our Lady of Mount Carmel is the best known of the small scapulars. Confraternity members share in the good works of the Carmelite Order. Pope St. Pius X officially decreed that in place of the cloth scapular one might wear a scapular medal. The feast commemorates the favors granted by our Lady on Mount Carmel and was extended to the Universal Church in 1726 by Benedict XIII.

THE CHURCH SPEAKS

PLACED by the grace of God, as God's Mother, next to her Son, and exalted above all angels and men, Mary intervened in the mysteries of Christ and is justly honored by a special cult in the Church. Clearly from earliest times the Blessed Virgin is honored under the title of Mother of God, under whose protection the faithful took refuge in all their dangers and necessities. Hence after the Synod of Ephesus the cult of the People of God toward Mary wonderfully increased in veneration and love, in invocation and imitation, according to her own prophetic words: "All generations shall call me blessed, because He Who is mighty has done great things for me" (Lk 1:48).

This cult, as it always existed, although it is altogether singular, differs essentially from the cult of adoration which is offered to the Incarnate Word, as well as to the Father and the Holy Spirit, and it is most favorable to it.

The various forms of piety toward the Mother of God—which the Church within the limits of sound and orthodox doctrine, according to the conditions of time and place, and the nature and ingenuity of the faithful has approved—bring it about that while the Mother is honored, the Son, through Whom all things have their being and in Whom it has pleased the Father that all fullness should dwell, is rightly known, loved and glorified and that all His commands are observed.

(Vatican II: *Constitution on the Church*, 66)

We view with great sympathy the distress our people feel over the loss of devotion to our Lady and we share their concern that the young be taught a deep and true love for the Mother of God. We Bishops of the United States wish to affirm with all our strength the lucid statements of the Second Vatican Council on the permanent importance of authentic devotion to the Blessed Virgin, not only in the liturgy, where the Church accords her a most special place under Jesus her Son, but also in the beloved devotions that have been repeatedly approved and encouraged by the Church and that are still filled with meaning for Catholics. As Pope Paul has reminded us, the rosary and the scapular are among these tested forms of devotion that bring us closer to Christ through the example and protection of His Holy Mother.

(*Behold Your Mother*, 93)

PRAYER

MARY, Mother of God, *you are our true Mother because you have given us super-natural life.* The supernatural life is the life of Jesus in us through grace. You have given us Christ that He may make us live of His life.

By consenting to give natural life to Jesus, you consented to give us supernatural life. In becoming His Mother, you became ours. From that hour, we were members of the Mystical Body of Christ. I thank you for consenting to become my spiritual Mother by giving me Jesus. Through your prayers, may Jesus make me live for His life through sanctifying and actual grace.

By His death Jesus merited for us the grace to live His life. He did this in union with you. You conceived Him as victim; you prepared Him for this sacrifice; beneath the cross you offered Him to the Father for our salvation. Jesus proclaimed your motherhood from the cross by entrusting you to John and John to you when He said, "Woman, behold, your son. . . . Behold, your Mother."

Mary, *you are more truly our Mother than any other mother by the way in which you have given us life.* To bring us forth, you gave much more than our earthly mothers gave. You bore unspeakable sufferings and offered the life of Him Who was dearer to you than your own life.

You love me with a love that is greater than the love of my own mother; you love me with the very love with which you love Jesus, since all your children form but one Body with Him. I thank you for all you mean to me as my spiritual Mother. During my whole life continue to take care of me until Christ be formed in me. If unfortunately I should lose this life by sin, bring me back to supernatural life. Make me more earnest in striving to grow in this divine life. Only then can I really love you as you desire—when Jesus is formed in me so that I can love you as Jesus does.

Mary, *I honor you under the title of Our Lady of Mount Carmel.* Remember me in my needs, and show yourself my Mother. Shed upon me more and more the living light of that faith which made you blessed. Inflame me with that heavenly love with which you loved your dear Son, Jesus Christ. Obtain for me from Jesus the gifts of humility, chastity, and meekness, which were the fairest adornments of your immaculate soul. Make me strong in the midst of the temptations and bitterness which sometimes trouble my soul. And when the days of my earthly pilgrimage are over, according to God's holy will, grant that my soul may obtain the glory of heaven, through the merits of Christ and through your intercession.

LITURGICAL PRAYER

FATHER,
    may the prayers of the Virgin Mary pro-
      tect us
and help us to reach Christ her Son
Who lives and reigns with You and the Holy
  Spirit,
one God, forever. Amen.

Additional prayers: pp. 172, 180.

DEDICATION OF ST. MARY MAJOR

August 5 (Triduum: August 2-4)

DOCTRINE

THE most celebrated shrine of our Lady in Rome is the Major Basilica of Saint Mary Major, which has its own feast day under the title of Our Lady of the Snows.

The Basilica was built on the Esquiline Hill by a wealthy Roman and his wife during the pontificate of Pope Liberius (352-356). They were guided in their choice of a site by the command of our Lady who appeared to them in a dream, and the subsequent miraculous fall of snow in midsummer confided to this particular hilltop. The snow is said to have covered a piece of ground of the form and size of a large church.

Later, on the occasion of the General Council of Ephesus, at which the Blessed Virgin was declared to be truly the Mother of God, Pope Sixtus III (432-440) rebuilt this Basilica and greatly enriched it in honor of the event. Thus the Basilica of Saint Mary Major became one of the four chief basilicas of the Eternal City.

A few years later the same church was enriched with a famous relic, the manger from the stable of Bethlehem; hence it is also called St. Mary at the Crib. No other shrine of our Lady has been visited by so many Popes, princes, and prelates in the history of the Church. It was the favorite shrine of Pope St. Gregory the Great.

This feast is a reminder that we should do all we can to contribute to the honor of the Blessed Virgin Mary. She is honored by the little things we do for her out of childlike love and she will repay us most generously.

THE CHURCH SPEAKS

THIS most Holy Synod deliberately teaches this Catholic doctrine and at the same time admonishes all the sons of the Church that the cult, especially the liturgical cult, of the Blessed Virgin, be generously fostered, and the practices and exercises of piety, recommended by the magisterium of the Church toward her in the course of centuries, be made of great moment, and those decrees, which have been given in the early days regarding the cult of images of Christ, the Blessed Virgin and the saints, be religiously observed. . . .

Let the faithful remember moreover that true devotion consists neither in sterile or transitory affection, nor in a certain vain credulity, but proceeds from true faith, by which we are led to know the excellence of the Mother of God, and we are moved to a filial love toward our Mother and to the imitation of her virtues.

(Vatican II: *Constitution on the Church*, 67)

What is the positive value of Mary's role as Mediatrix, and how does she exercise it? The Gospels portray her as a woman who walked by faith from the time of the Annunciation to Pentecost. The Virgin of Nazareth belonged to a family circle that was awaiting the consolation of Israel (Lk 2:5). The Mother of Jesus appears as totally responsive to the Father's will, always one with her Son's purposes, led by the Holy Spirit in everything. "Be it done unto me according to your word" (Lk 1:38) was the act of faith of the Lord's handmaid, a sign of her unwavering service to God in every detail of her life.

In the Scriptures, "faith" means surrender of heart and body as well as of mind and intellect. St. Luke writes of Mary "reflecting in her heart" (Lk 2:19, 51). St. John records the advice she exemplified in her own life: "Do whatever He tells you" (Jn 2:5). The Gospels provide few details of Mary's life; but they do delineate a remarkable portrait of the woman who gave herself wholeheartedly to her Son and His mission in perfect faith, love and obedience. What Mary began on earth in association with the saving mission of Jesus, she continues still, in union with the risen Christ.

(Behold Your Mother, 69)

PRAYER

MARY, Mother of God, *you are also the Mother of men.* You conceived Jesus as the Head of regenerated mankind, the Head of a Mystical Body whose members we are. You also conceived His members who have been born again and are called to incorporation with Him. When you became the Mother of Jesus according to the flesh, you became the Mother of men according to the Spirit. This truth was confirmed on Calvary when, at the very moment our redemption was to be completed by the death of Jesus, He said to you, "Woman, behold, your son," then to John, who took our place beneath the cross, "Behold, your Mother." This was a declaration that all Christians are your spiritual children.

I am happy to be your child. As the surest refuge for a child is the heart of its mother, so you are my refuge. In His infancy Jesus depended upon your loving care, and in death when He was abandoned by many, He still had you. The last beat of His Heart was to be one with yours just as the first had been. I appeal to you for help. I trust that through you I shall obtain the help I need to keep the commandments, avoid sin, receive the Sacraments frequently, pray much, and save my soul.

Mary, *you are my model of perfect dedication to God.* Holiness is union with God through love. Through love you consecrated yourself with all your powers to God, the highest form of beauty and goodness. You knew nothing but God and His love; you wished for nothing but Him and His holy will; you sought nothing but His greater honor. This intimacy with God was the soul of your soul—your very life.

God enriched your soul with such a love above all other creatures that in you He found His delight as He did in Jesus. Your soul was most beautiful, lovable, and immaculate, rich in graces and virtues. The Holy Spirit, Who in virtue of your Son's merits lived in you, made you a living image of Jesus. Never were you guilty of the least fault; never did you offer the least resistance to grace. You are the model of all virtues. As I gaze upon you—the ideal of holiness—may a similar longing for God and complete dedication of myself to Him awaken in my soul.

God's grace can also do wonders in me if only I do not refuse to cooperate with it. May looking upon you inspire confidence in me which will make me more eager to grow in holiness. And I am sure there is nothing you want more than to see me perfectly dedicated to God even as you are. Since this is the mission of your life, to bring souls to God through Jesus, lead me to your loving Son. Only give me the grace to abandon myself completely to your motherly guidance.

Mary, *I consecrate myself to you.* Teach me to understand that personal consecration to you does not mean only to place myself under your special protection, but rather to live for God in union with you by avoiding every sin and by practicing virtue. I realize that imitating you is the best way of imitating Jesus and of obtaining your powerful intercession.

I want to be devoted to you by giving myself entirely to you and through you to God. In doing so I simply imitate God Who gave Himself and His Son to us through you. I give you my intellect by holding you in loving reverence because of your dignity as Mother of God. I give you my will by an absolute confidence in you, a confidence founded on your power and your goodness. I give you my heart by the gift of a tender and childlike love, because you are my Mother and you love me more than my own mother could ever think of loving me. I give you my whole being by imitating as far as possible all your virtues. I ask through your intercession the graces I need in order to imitate you and to go through you to Jesus.

LITURGICAL PRAYER

L ORD, pardon the sins of Your people. Since by ourselves we cannot please You, may the prayers of Mary, the Mother of Your Son,
help to bring us to salvation.
Grant this through our Lord Jesus Christ, Your Son,
Who lives and reigns with You and the Holy Spirit,
one God, forever. Amen.

Additional prayers: pp. 186, 188.

All generations shall call me blessed

ASSUMPTION OF THE B.V.M.

August 15 (Novena: August 6-14)

DOCTRINE

THE Assumption is the most ancient and solemn of all the feasts which Holy Church celebrates in honor of the Mother of God. It is the fulfillment of all the other great mysteries by which her life was made most wonderful.

The term *Assumption* means three things, namely, the death of the Blessed Virgin, her resurrection soon after death, and her entrance—body and soul—into heaven. At the present time the word is used exclusively to designate the Blessed Virgin's entrance into heaven, body and soul. It is used in contrast to Ascension, which signifies our Lord's bodily entrance into heaven of His own divine power. His Mother's Assumption was due solely to the power of Almighty God.

This belief of Catholics is founded on authentic teaching dating back certainly to the 6th century.

This teaching is drawn from tradition, authority, Scriptural comparisons, and the sense of what was fitting for the Mother who gave to Christ His Body and Blood.

One of the earliest feasts we know of in memory of the Virgin Mary was kept at Antioch about the year 380. It commemorated the death of the Blessed Mother. In the 6th century there is mention of a solemn feast of Mary which is believed to have been the Assumption.

A doctrine, universally held for over thirteen hundred years, could only have originated in a special revelation of our Lord and his Apostles. The Assumption of our Lady was defined at Rome, November 1, 1950, by Pope Pius XII: "By the authority of our Lord Jesus Christ, of the blessed Apostles Peter and Paul, and by Our own authority, We pronounce, declare, and define it to be a divinely revealed dogma: that the Immaculate Mother of God, Mary, ever-Virgin, after her life on earth, was assumed, body and soul, into heavenly glory."

We should unite our joy and gratitude with that of the angels and saints in heaven as well as that of the Church upon earth, for it is our Heavenly Mother's Coronation Day. How well did she deserve this immortal crown! She crushed the serpent's head. She offered herself and her beloved Son unto death for the redemption of mankind. She triumphed over the world and the devil. Let us pray that Mary may reign as Queen in our hearts.

THE CHURCH SPEAKS

THIS maternity of Mary in the order of grace began with the consent which she gave in faith at the Annunciation and which she sustained without wavering beneath the cross, and lasts until the eternal fulfillment of all the elect. Taken up to heaven she did not lay aside this salvific duty, but by her constant intercession continued to bring us the gifts of eternal salvation. By her maternal charity, she cares for the brethren of her Son, who still journey on earth surrounded by dangers and difficulties, until they are led into the happiness of their true home.

Therefore the Blessed Virgin is invoked by the Church under the titles of Advocate, Auxiliatrix, Adjutrix, and Mediatrix. This, however, is to be so understood that it neither takes away from nor adds anything to the dignity and efficaciousness of Christ the one Mediator.

(Vatican II: *Constitution on the Church*, 62)

As early as the 5th century, Christians celebrated a "Memorial of Mary," patterned on the "birthday into heaven" of the martyrs' anniversaries. By this they gave prayer form to their belief in the resurrection of the body and in the special bond between holy Mary and Jesus, the risen Savior. This primitive "Memorial of Mary," sometimes observed on August 15, evolved into the feast of the Dormition (the "falling asleep") of the Virgin.

As early as the 6th century, homilies on the Assumption appear, which bring out the abiding and perfect conformity of the Mother of Jesus with "her Son, the Lord of lords, and the Conqueror of sin and death." An 8th century prayer, originally an announcement of a procession on August 15, has survived as an entrance prayer in some Western liturgies (e.g., the Carmelite rite until recently): "On this day the holy Mother of God suffered temporal death, but could not be held fast by the bonds of death, who gave birth to our Lord made flesh."

United to the victorious Christ in heaven, Mary is "the image and first-flowering of the Church as she is to be perfected in the world to come." She shines forth "as a sign of sure hope and solace for the pilgrim People of God." In her Assumption, Mary manifests the fullness of redemption, and appears as the "spotless image" of the Church responding in joy to the invitation of the Bridegroom Christ, Himself the "first fruits of those who have fallen asleep" (1 Cor 15:20).

Christ has risen from the dead; we need no further assurance of our faith. "Mary assumed into heaven" serves rather as a gracious reminder to the Church that our Lord wishes all whom the Father has given Him to be raised with Him. In Mary taken to glory, to union with Christ, the Church sees herself answering the invitation of the heavenly Bridegroom.

(Behold Your Mother, 57-60)

PRAYER

MARY, Mother of God, *your death was accompanied by three graces that made it precious and full of joy.* You died as you had lived, entirely detached from the things of the world; you died in the most perfect peace and in the certainty of eternal glory.

Your Son, though He was Life itself, did not exempt Himself from death. So, as daughter of Adam you submitted to the sentence passed in the garden of Eden. You died of no infirmity. Intense love for the Infinite God withdrew your soul from this earthly life.

Though your body was separated from your soul in death, your soul was reunited in your incorrupt body, and you were taken up into heaven by angels. The bodies of even the just are corrupted after death, and only on the last day will they be joined, each to its own glorious soul. But God has willed that you should be exempted from this general rule because, by an entirely singular privilege, you completely overcame sin by your Immaculate Conception.

Corruption is a consequence of sin, but you were sinless. You did not have to wait until the end of time for the resurrection of your body. As the body of your Divine Son was preserved from the corruption of the grave, so you, from whom He took flesh, were also free from the power of earthly decay. Your body, which was the living tabernacle of the Eternal God and the temple of the Adorable Trinity, was not meant to crumble into dust.

Mary, *I believe that you, the Immaculate Mother of God, having completed the course of your earthly life, were assumed body and soul into heavenly glory.* Jesus ascended into heaven by His own power as Lord and Creator, accompanied by angels who paid Him homage. You were taken to heaven by the power of God, accompanied and upheld by the angels, raised aloft by grace, not by nature.

Jesus ascended to heaven before you not only that He might prepare a throne for you in that kingdom, but also that He might Himself accompany you with all the blessed spirits and thus render your entry into heaven more glorious and worthy of His Mother. At the Annunciation you received Jesus on earth; it was proper that He should receive you in heaven. Having deigned to come down to you, He wished to raise you up to Himself in order that you might enter into glory.

The day of your Assumption was the great day of your triumph. In your triumph, as the Mother of the Word of God Incarnate, having perfectly followed out the great designs of God upon you, having acquired immense merits by the practice of all the virtues, and having reached the highest holiness, you were assumed body and soul into heaven. Angels came to escort you. You were born aloft to the palace of your beloved Son.

You passed amid the different choirs of the blessed, above all the heavenly spirits, and approached the throne of light prepared for you. Your loving Son welcomed you with joy. What songs of gladness by the elect as you were crowned by the Blessed Trinity and made Queen of Heaven, advocate of the human race, and dispenser of the graces of the Redemption!

Mary, *you reign in splendor for all eternity with your Divine Son.* Your kingdom, like His, is a kingdom of imperishable glory, because yours is a throne of clemency, mercy, and pardon. All your trials and sufferings are now transformed into jewels that decorate your triumphal throne in heaven.

I can only faintly imagine with what tenderness the Eternal Father received you, His loving Daughter; the Divine Son, His chosen Mother; and the Holy Spirit, His immaculate

Bride. The Three Divine Persons declared you Queen of heaven and earth and assigned to you a place at the right hand of Jesus. You received from the Adorable Trinity the crown and scepter, which made you Queen of all the angels and saints and the all-powerful Mediatrix between God and men. You became the channel through which He dispenses His gifts upon earth.

Your Assumption was not only the crowning of a holy life for you, but also a cause of joy and triumph for the human race. Your Assumption, together with the Ascension of Jesus, became for mortal man a sure pledge of resurrection and immortality.

I wish to recall this triumph and to share in your glory. If the honor of parents descends upon their children, what joy for all of us, your children, to see you raised to such heights of glory! Confidence fills my soul, for you were raised to this glory not for your own advantage only, but for that of your children also, in order to make us feel the effects of your powerful protection and intercession.

One of your greatest delights is to lavish these treasures upon your faithful children. With your arms outstretched—those arms in which the Eternal God delighted to rest when He became our Brother—plead our cause. Pray to Him for us, your children, that

in our exile we may resemble you, His most
devoted follower, and at last may glorify Him
in union with you forever.

HYMN

WHEN for me the sun is setting
At the close of life's brief day;
When my little ship is nearing
Port in yonder crystal bay;
Then, O my beloved Mother,
Stretch thy kind hand out to me,
Shield me, till my feet have touch'd the
Shore sand of eternity.

When my strength begins to vanish,
And earth's memories to fade;
When my friends stand sad and silent,
Powerless to give me aid;
Then, my beloved Mother,
Hold my trembling hand in thine,
Till my eyes shall see the steeples
Of the Holy City shine.

When at last my weary spirit
Seeks admission to thy throne,
When my lips in anxious longing
For thy gracious blessing moan!
Then, O thrice beloved Mother,
Open wide thy home and heart,
And let me, thy child, dwell ever,
Where thou Queen and Mother art.

LITURGICAL PRAYER

ALL-POWERFUL and ever-living God,
You raised the sinless Virgin Mary,
Mother of Your Son,
body and soul to the glory of heaven.
May we ever look toward heaven as our final
  home
and come to share her glory.
We ask this through our Lord Jesus Christ,
  Your Son,
Who lives and reigns with You and the Holy
  Spirit,
one God, forever. Amen.

Additional prayer: 199.

come out of the mouth of the Most High

QUEENSHIP OF MARY

August 22 (Novena: August 13-21)

DOCTRINE

ACCORDING to ancient tradition and the sacred liturgy, *the main principle on which the royal dignity of Mary rests is her Divine Motherhood.* The Archangel Gabriel spoke to Mary concerning the Son Whom she would conceive: "Behold you will conceive in your womb and bear a Son, and you will name Him Jesus. He will be great and will be called Son of the Most High. The Lord God will give Him the throne of His ancestor David. He will rule over the house of Jacob forever, and of His kingdom there will be no end" (Lk 1:31-32). Elizabeth calls her "the mother of my Lord." Hence Mary is a Queen, since she bore a Son Who, at the very moment of His conception, because of the hypostatic union of the human nature with the Word, was also as man King and Lord of all things. The heavenly voice of the archangel was the first to proclaim Mary's royal office.

Furthermore, *God has willed Mary to have an exceptional role in the work of our eternal salvation.*

Now, in the accomplishing of this work of redemption, the Blessed Virgin Mary was most closely associated with Christ. Just as Jesus, because he redeemed us, is our King by a special title, so the Blessed Virgin also is our Queen on account of the unique manner in which she assisted in our redemption, by giving of her own substance, by freely offering Him for us, by her singular desire and petition for, and active interest in, our salvation.

Mary is the new Eve. A Virgin was instrumental in the salvation of the human race, just as Eve was closely associated with its death. As Christ, the new Adam, must be called a King not only because He is Son of God, but also because He is our Redeemer, so the Blessed Virgin is Queen not only because she is Mother of God, but also because, as the new Eve, she was associated with the new Adam, for she had been chosen Mother of Christ in order that she might become a partner in the redemption of the human race.

Pope Pius XII published an encyclical letter, *Ad Caeli Reginam,* on the Royal Dignity of the Blessed Virgin Mary and on the institution of her feast, on October 11, 1954. From ancient Christian documents, from prayers of the Liturgy, from the spontaneous piety of the Christian people, from works of art, he gathered proofs of the queenly dignity of the Blessed Virgin Mary. He likewise showed that the arguments deduced by sacred theology confirm this truth.

Mary, as Mother of the Divine Christ, as His associate in the Redemption, in His struggle with His enemies and His final victory over them, has a share, though in a limited way, in His royal dignity. From her union with Christ she attains a radiant eminence surpassing that of any other creature. From her union with Christ she receives the royal right to dispose of the treasures of the Divine Redeemer's Kingdom. From her union with Christ is derived the power of her motherly intercession before the Son and His Father.

The sublime dignity of the Mother of God over all creatures can be better understood if we recall that Mary was, at the very moment of her Immaculate Conception, so filled with grace as to surpass the grace of all the saints. Besides, the Blessed Virgin possessed, after Christ, not only the highest degree of excellence and perfection, but also a share in that influence by which He, her Son and our Redeemer, is rightly said to reign over the minds and wills of men. For if through His humanity the Divine Word performs miracles and gives graces, if He uses His sacraments and saints as instruments for the salvation of men, why should He not make use of the role and work of His most holy Mother in imparting to us the fruits of redemption?

Mary intercedes powerfully for us with a mother's prayers; she obtains what she seeks, and cannot be refused, for almost immeasurable power has been given to her in the distribution of graces. We should glory in being subjects of the Virgin Mother of God, who, while wielding royal power, is on fire with a mother's love.

THE CHURCH SPEAKS

BY REASON of the gift and role of divine maternity, by which she is united with her Son, the Redeemer, and with His singular graces and functions, the Blessed Virgin is also intimately united with the Church. As St. Ambrose taught, the Mother of God is a type of the Church in the order of faith, charity, and perfect union with Christ. For in the mystery of the Church (which is itself rightly called mother and virgin), the Blessed Virgin stands out in eminent and singular fashion as exemplar both of virgin and mother.

By her belief and obedience, not knowing man but overshadowed by the Holy Spirit, as the new Eve she brought forth on earth the very Son of the Father, showing an undefiled faith, not in the word of the ancient serpent, but in that of God's messenger. The Son Whom she brought forth is He Whom God placed as the first-born among many brethren, namely, the faithful, in whose birth and education she cooperates with a maternal love.

The Church indeed, contemplating her hidden sanctity, imitating her charity and faithfully fulfilling the Father's will, by receiving the Word of God in faith becomes herself a mother. By her preaching she brings forth to a new and immortal life the sons who are born to her in baptism, conceived of the Holy Spirit and born of God. She herself is a virgin, who keeps the faith given to her by her Spouse whole and entire. Imitating the Mother of her Lord, and by the power of the Holy Spirit, she keeps with virginal purity an entire faith, a firm hope, and a sincere charity.

(Vatican II: *Constitution on the Church*, 63, 64)

In this title, the "Church," of which Mary is Mother, is seen as comprising both shepherds and flocks, both pastors and people. As a believing disciple of Jesus, Mary can be called daughter of the Church, and our sister as well. For, like us, she has been redeemed by Christ, although in an eminent and privileged way. What is the special significance of the title "Mother of the Church"? It is based on Mary's being the Mother of God. By God's call and her free response in the power of His grace, Mary became the Mother of Jesus, Son of God made man, and thus truly "Mother of God."

She remained joined to her Son's saving work in the new economy in which He freed men from sin by the mysteries of His flesh. On Calvary, Jesus gave John into Mary's care and thus designated her Mother of the human race which the beloved disciple represented. At the Annunciation, Mary conceived Christ by the power of the Holy Spirit. After Christ's Resurrection, surrounded by His disciples, Mary prayed for the coming of that same Spirit, in order that the Church, the Body of her Son, might be born on Pentecost. Through her faith and love, Mary's maternity reached out to include all the members of her Son's Mystical Body.

Her union with the risen Lord has added to Mary's motherhood of the Church a new effectiveness, as she shares in the everlasting intercession of our great High Priest. In calling Mary "Mother of the Church," we are reminded that she is also the Mother of unity, sharing her Son's desire and prayer that His Body be truly one. It is encouraging to note that some members of other Christian Churches found in Pope Paul's title, Mother of the Church, a sign of ecumenical hope.

The basic reason why Mary is Mother of the Church is that she is Mother of God, and the associate of Christ in His saving work. Another great reason is that the Mother of Jesus "shines as the model of virtues for the whole community of the elect." As Pope Paul put it, "Jesus gave us Mary as our Mother, and proposed her as a model to be imitated." The Mother of Jesus exemplified in her own life the beatitudes preached by her Son, and so the Church, in and through the many activities of its various members and vocations, rightly regards Mary, Mother of the Church, as the perfect model of the imitation of Christ.

(Behold Your Mother, 114-117)

PRAYER

MARY, Mother of God, I believe that as Mediatrix with Jesus you share also in His sovereign dominion over the universe. *You are Queen because you are the Mother of the Word Incarnate.* Christ is universal King because He rules all creatures by His personal union with the Divinity. You brought Him into the world that He might be King, according to the words of the archangel, "And of His kingdom there will be no end."

You are Queen also b*ecause you are core-demptrix.* Jesus reigns over us not only by natural right, but also by the right of redemption. As cooperator with your Son in that work of redemption, you also acquired the right to reign with Him. God chose you to be His Mother and by that very choice has associated you with Himself in the work of the salvation of men.

Since you had your place beside Jesus when there was question of ransoming us and meriting for us all the graces necessary for our salvation, you must in like manner have your place beside Him now, when there is question of securing for us by your prayers in heaven the graces prepared for us in view of the merits of Christ. This is my hope: that you will be a mother to me and obtain for me the grace I need to save my soul.

Mary, *yours is a queenship of goodness.* You add a degree of motherly sweetness to the joy of the angels and saints and to the blessed of the Church triumphant. To the Church suffering you bring consolation, relief, deliverance; to the Church militant you offer aid, confidence, victory.

Yours is *a queenship of dominion.* You exercise your queenly dominion over the minds, the hearts, the wills, and even over the bodies of your subjects. You rule over their minds by making them understand better the teaching of Christ; over their hearts, by turning them to Jesus through the charm of your motherly affection; over their wills, by gently inclining them to observe all the commandments of your Son; over their bodies, by teaching men to subject their members to the law of God through the practice of temperance and chastity. The more fully you are Queen in a soul, the more does Jesus reign there as King. Reign over my mind and heart and will and body so that I may belong completely to Jesus through you.

Yours is *a queenship of conquest.* How many souls have still to be brought under the rule of Christ the King! Fulfill your apostolic mission of winning the world for Christ. As formerly the shepherds and the Magi found Jesus close to you, so now may all sinners, unbelievers, and pagans find Jesus through you, His Mother. Hasten the reign of Christ by ruling over all of us, your children.

Mary, from your heart we hope to obtain the love of God that He expects from His creatures, and also the pardon that guilty but repentant creatures ask from their merciful Creator. All souls belong to you and your Son. He is King and you are Queen of all hearts. Rule over us by the queenly power of your love that the Kingdom of your Son—the Kingdom of Truth and Life, Holiness and Grace, Justice, Love, and Peace—may come upon earth.

HYMN

MARY, Queen of Heaven, star on life's dark sea,
All our hearts are given, Virgin pure, to thee.
Life and land and nation at thy feet today
All in consecration joyfully we lay.

Queen of God's creation, Spouse of God's fair love,
Peerless is thy station with thy Son above.
In thy pure maternal hands our own we press;
Lead us to eternal heaven's happiness.

Well we know the kindness, shining in thy eyes,
From our sinful blindness thou wilt help us rise.
Earth can claim no other, Virgin, like to thee;
Ever blessed Mother, hear thy children's plea!

LITURGICAL PRAYER

FATHER,
You have given us the Mother of Your Son
to be our Queen and Mother.
With the help of her prayers
may we come to share the glory of Your children
in the kingdom of heaven.
We ask this through our Lord Jesus Christ,
Your Son,
Who lives and reigns with You and the Holy
Spirit,
one God, forever. Amen.

Additional prayers: pp. 177, 203.

The Lord begot me the first born of His ways

SEPTEMBER

NATIVITY OF
THE BLESSED VIRGIN MARY

September 8 (Novena: August 30-September 7)

DOCTRINE

ACCORDING to an ancient tradition the parents of the Blessed Virgin were Joachim and Ann. Nothing historically trustworthy is known about Joachim and Ann, but they must have been persons of superior sanctity. We may rest assured that God would have chosen parents worthy to educate a child of such high destiny and singular holiness. For a long time they were without children. God rewarded their prayers and granted them a daughter. There cannot be any doubt that Mary was of Davidic lineage, at least through Joachim, and perhaps through Ann as well. The bodily origin of the Messiah from David had been predicted by Isaiah (11:1). Joachim and Ann named their daughter Miriam, after the valiant sister of Moses.

Because the Annunciation took place at Nazareth and because most of Mary's relatives resided there, she was most probably born in that village, situated in the hill country of southern Galilee. According to tradition, the house where Mary was born was located on the site where the Basilica of the Annunciation now stands. This is built over some caves, one of which is venerated as the scene of the Annunciation.

Mary was chosen from all eternity to give us the Savior; hence she was eternally in God's plan of Redemption. In time she was immaculately conceived and her birth brought salvation to mankind. Next to Christmas, there is no other birthday so happy and so important as the birthday of Mary the Mother of God. The world sees for the first time a human being who is free of every stain of sin from the beginning of her existence.

This very ancient feast was already solemnized in the 7th century. This date served to fix that of the Immaculate Conception on December 8th.

We should thank God for having created this most beautiful of creatures and for having given her to us as a Mother. We should thank Him for all the mercies He has shown to mankind through Mary. Our birthday gift to our heavenly Mother should be the wholehearted consecration of ourselves to her.

THE CHURCH SPEAKS

WISHING in His supreme goodness and wisdom to effect the redemption of the world, "when the fullness of time came, God sent His Son, born of a woman . . . that we might receive the adoption of sons (Gal 4:4-7)." "He for us men, and for our salvation, came down from heaven, and was incarnate by the Holy Spirit from the Virgin Mary." This divine mystery of salvation is revealed to us and continued in the Church, which the Lord established as His Body. Joined to Christ the Head and in the unity of fellowship with all His saints, the faithful must in the first place reverence the memory "of the glorious ever Virgin Mary, Mother of God and Lord Jesus Christ."

(Vatican II: *Constitution on the Church*, 52)

Mary is Queen of the home. As a woman of faith, she inspires all mothers to transmit the Christian faith to their children. In the setting of family love, children should learn free and loving obedience, inspired by Mary's obedience, to God. Her example of concern for others, as shown at the wedding feast of Cana, will exercise its gentle influence. "He went down with them . . and was obedient to them. . . . [Jesus] progressed steadily in wisdom and age and grace before God and men" (Lk 2:51-52). This obedience of Jesus is emphasized throughout the New Testament: at Nazareth, throughout His ministry in which He sought only to do His Father's will, even unto death.

The Gospel makes clear also Mary's obedience to the Law and to the traditional prayer life of her people. This is evident, for example, in her annual trip to Jerusalem for the Passover. Faithful to the Law of Moses, the holy couple brought Jesus to the Temple, His Father's house, for the presentation. Such obedience was the flower of Mary's faith. Because of it, God found her worthy to be the Mother of His Son.

In her appearances during the public life, Mary showed the same generous response to the will of the Father made manifest in her Son. At the marriage feast of Cana, after her Son's mysterious reference to the "hour not yet come," Mary's reaction was to advise the waiter, "Do whatever He tells you" (Jn 2:5). Family love builds on the fourth Commandment, and in Jesus, Mary, and Joseph, parents and children have a powerful example of obedience to the will of God.

Family prayer, in whatever form it takes—meal prayers, night prayers, the family rosary, attending Mass together—provides opportunities for prayers to the Blessed Virgin. Children forget many things when they grow up. They do not forget the manly piety of the father, the gentle devotion of the mother, and love of Jesus and Mary as the Support of the home, in sorrow and in joy.

(*Behold Your Mother*, 137-139)

PRAYER

MARY, Mother of God, *you are the Virgin who was promised as the mother of the Savior.* After the fall of our First Parents, earth, which was to be Paradise, was changed into a valley of tears on which the curse of God fell. People became the poor banished children of Eve. They roamed about in the darkness of sin and despair. In his infinite mercy God chose Abraham who was to be the father of a chosen nation. You were descended from the most renowned men of that nation and counted among your ancestors patriarchs, prophets, leaders of the people of God, and kings of the ancient Law. Your birth was represented beforehand by many figures, announced by prophets, desired for many ages by the human race.

Prophets foretold the coming of the Savior and the manner in which the Redemption would take place. They spoke of you as His Virgin Mother and of the part you would play in the Redemption of mankind. Balaam referred to you as a star: "The star that shall arise from Jacob." Isaiah called you a Virgin: "The Virgin will be with child, and she will give birth to a son, and she will call Him Immanuel."

Your birth was awaited as the near sign of the deliverance of the human race. The

Church regards you as the rising dawn. As the dawn precedes and announces the coming of the sun, makes the darkness of the night disappear, consoles the sick and rejoices all nature, so you went before and announced Jesus, "the Sun of Justice," Who made the darkness of the world disappear by the light of His Gospel, consoled and cured the sick in soul and body, and brought an abundance of graces and blessings to the whole world.

Mary, at the very beginning of your existence *you received grace exceeding in greatness that of all the saints* because you were destined to be the Mother of the Redeemer and the Mediatrix of the world. From the first instant of your existence your mind was filled by the supernatural light of faith and your soul with love of God. Who can describe the grace that adorned your soul at the glorious instant of your nativity! Your soul had never been touched by original sin. With my whole heart I thank God for all He has done for you and for all mankind through you.

Mary, *your dear parents, Joachim and Ann, rejoiced at your birth.* I admire the holiness of their lives and the nobility of their family. They observed the Law of God most diligently and spent their days in prayer and in works of mercy.

Only after many years of fervent prayers did God reward your parents. You were born into the world at Nazareth. Your birth was a miracle of the power of God because both of your parents were far advanced in years. Who could tell the great joy which filled their hearts when they held you in their arms! But all heaven rejoiced at your birth, because you were destined one day to bring the Savior into the world; you were to become God's Mother and the Queen of heaven and earth.

I rejoice with the Blessed Trinity on your birthday because you were to take part in the Incarnation and Redemption of the world. I rejoice with all mankind because you became the Mother of our Redeemer. I rejoice with the whole Church because you are our life: you bore Jesus, Who is the Way and the Truth and the Life, and Who was to restore to mankind that supernatural life which had been lost. I have every reason to rejoice, for as the Mother of Jesus and my Mother, you are my hope of salvation. Through your prayers and the prayers of your holy parents may I learn to know and love you more and ever remain your faithful child. This is my sure way of reaching heaven and my God.

HYMN

DAUGHTER of the mighty Father,
Maiden, heaven's brightest ray,

Angel forms around you gather,
Dawn of earth's Eternal Day!

Mother of the Son and Savior
Of the Truth, the Life, the Way,
Guide our footsteps, calm our passions,
Dawn of earth's Eternal Day!

Spouse of the Eternal Spirit,
Blossom which will ne'er decay,
Let us but your love inherit,
Dawn of earth's Eternal Day!

Daughter, Mother, Spouse of Heaven,
Hearken to our earnest lay,
Sweetest gift to man e'er given,
Dawn of earth's Eternal Day.

LITURGICAL PRAYER

FATHER of mercy,
give Your people help and strength from
heaven.
Since the birth of the Virgin Mary's Son
was the dawn of our salvation,
may this celebration of her birthday
bring us closer to lasting peace.
Grant this through our Lord Jesus Christ, Your
Son,
Who lives and reigns with You and the Holy
Spirit,
one God, forever. Amen.

Additional prayer: p. 172.

OUR LADY OF SORROWS

September 15 (Novena: September 6-14)

DOCTRINE

THE seven sorrows of the Blessed Virgin Mary that have made the strongest appeal to devotion are: the prophecy of Simeon, the flight into Egypt, the three days' loss of Jesus, the meeting with Jesus carrying His cross, His death on Calvary, His being taken down from the cross, and His burial in the tomb.

Simeon foretold to the Mother the opposition the Redeemer would arouse, and the sword that was to pierce her own heart, "You yourself a sword will pierce." Mary's sorrow on Calvary was deeper than any sorrow ever felt on earth, for no mother in all the world had a heart as tender as the heart of the Mother of God. As there was no love like her love, there was no sorrow like her sorrow. She bore her sufferings for us that we might enjoy the graces of Redemption. She suffered willingly in order to prove her great love for us, for true love is proved by sacrifice.

It was not because she was the Mother of God that Mary could bear her sorrows, but because she saw things from His point of view and not from her own—or rather, she had made His point of view hers. We should do the same. The Mother of Sorrows will be on hand to help us.

Devotion to the sorrows of Mary is the source of great graces because it leads into the depths of the Heart of Christ. If we think frequently of the false pleasures of this world, we shall embrace patiently the sorrows and sufferings of this life, and we shall be penetrated with a sorrow for sin. The Church urges us to give ourselves over to her love completely and bear our cross patiently with the Mother of Sorrows.

THE CHURCH SPEAKS

IN THE public life of Jesus, Mary makes significant appearances. This is so even at the very beginning, when at the marriage feast of Cana, moved with pity, she brought about by her intercession the beginning of miracles of Jesus the Messiah. In the course of her Son's preaching she received the words whereby, in extolling a kingdom beyond the calculations and bonds of flesh and blood, He declared blessed those who heard and kept the Word of God, as she was faithfully doing.

After this manner, the Blessed Virgin advanced in her pilgrimage of faith, and faithfully persevered in her union with her Son unto the cross, where she stood, in keeping

with the divine plan, grieving exceedingly with
her only-begotten Son, uniting herself with a
maternal heart to His sacrifice, and lovingly
consenting to the immolation of this Victim
which she herself had brought forth. Finally,
she was given by the same Christ Jesus dying
on the cross as a mother to His disciple, with
these words: "Woman, behold your son."

(Vatican II: *Constitution on the Church*, 58)

As a perfect disciple, the Virgin Mary heard
the Word of God and kept it, to the lasting joy
of the messianic generations who call her
blessed. It is our Catholic conviction that in
her present union with the risen Christ, our
Blessed Mother is still solicitous for our welfare, still desirous that we become more like
Jesus, her first-born. The Mother of Jesus wishes all her other children, all men and all
women, to reach the maturity of the fullness of
Christ (Eph 4:13; Col 1:28).

Word of God—faith—birth of Christ: this
is the pattern for the maternity of Mary and
the maternity of the Church. Life is the dom-
inant note in the language of motherhood.
Mary brings forth Christ the Life; the Church
continually regenerates men in the Christ-life.
For both Mary and the Church, their motherhood is virginal, that is, entirely dependent on
God, not on man. The Church's mission as

"mother of the redeemed" was first realized in the Virgin Mother of Jesus. Open to the over-shadowing Spirit, as was the Virgin Mary, the Church receives the Word of God and brings forth life.

There are striking likenesses between the Annunciation and Pentecost. From the over-shadowing of the Spirit, Christ is conceived; from the Pentecostal outpouring of the Spirit, Christ is born in His members who are the Church. Mary, the great mother figure for the Church, is present not only at the Annunciation, but praying with her Son's disciples before Pentecost.

(Behold Your Mother, 78, 79)

PRAYER

MARY, Mother of God, *your sorrows were ordained by God from all eternity as part of the penalty to be paid for sin and were to mingle with the sufferings of your Son in that great sacrifice which was to redeem the world.*

The Gospel speaks of you as standing beneath the cross. Though your soul was filled with grief, you bravely stood beneath the cross. You did not abandon Jesus as the apostles did; you remained with Him until He expired. You drew near to the cross. You beheld Him suspended by iron nails. You stood there silently fulfilling a part assigned to you by Providence.

You were to complete the offering of your Son, which you had begun on the day of His presentation in the Temple. You presented Him in sacrifice to the Father as your God and the Son of Man, as your offering and the offering of humanity for the Redemption of the world. You so loved the world as to give your only Son for our Redemption.

You had to offer the most intense human suffering, in union with the Passion of your Son. You saw in the cross an altar, in your Son a priest, and in His blood the price of our Redemption. You suffered in your soul what Jesus suffered in His body, and in union with Him you offered yourself as a victim for our sins. You sanctified all our afflictions and united them with those of Jesus. I can never fully understand the depth of those sorrows that filled your heart as you begot us to the spiritual life, while standing by the cross on Calvary. The words of the prophet are applied to you: "O all you that pass by the way, attend, and see if there be sorrow like unto my sorrow."

Mary, *your life, like that of your Divine Son, was a daily crucifixion and martyrdom.* You found the cross very heavy during the three years of His public life. Though deprived of the joy of the presence of Jesus, you were more intimately united with Him than ever through your sacrificial love, since your will was one with His.

Because you freely consented to become the Mother of God, you experienced mentally all the bitterness of your Son's Passion and death. Though worn with sorrow, you took your place at the foot of the cross. You generously offered Jesus as a sacrifice to the justice of His offended Father. You united the oblation of your own suffering and grief with the offering of Jesus, thus proving yourself worthy not only to share but also to be one with Him in the redemption of souls.

Mary, *you are our spiritual Mother.* The crucifixion was not only the sacrifice for sin; it was also the new birth of mankind to the spiritual life, lost by the sin of Adam. It was the great vital act that completed the work of God in the world. You had a share in that work; it was part of your life work. The new birth of mankind was completed on Calvary. You were present as Mother of the human race, the New Eve.

Your dying Son declared this in His words to you from the cross, "Woman, behold, your son." Those words include us all. You were declared to be the spiritual "Mother of all the living." And when Jesus said to John, "Behold, your Mother," He wanted John to respect and to love you as his Mother. John took my place on Calvary and you became, in his person, my Mother. Jesus could give me— after the gift of Himself—nothing more precious than you. With your heart breaking with sorrow, you had to die a spiritual death in order to become my spiritual Mother.

Since you are my Mother, I share in the love you have for your Divine Son. I can best thank Jesus for His dying bequest by striving daily to become like John in his love and imitation of you. It means imitating your humility, your purity, your detachment from the world, and your unselfish resignation to the will of God in every event of life. It also means unlimited confidence in your motherly intercession. I give you my love by consecrating myself entirely to you, in joy and in sorrow, by complete abandonment to the will of God. I confide my salvation to your loving care. Keep me close to you now and at the hour of my death.

HYMN

O THOU Mother, fount of love!
Touch my spirit from above;
Make my heart with thine accord.
Make me feel as thou hast felt;
Make my soul to glow and melt
With the love of Christ our Lord.

Holy Mother, pierce me through;
In my heart each wound renew,
Of my Savior crucified!
Let me share with thee His pain,
Who for all my sins was slain,
Who for me in torments died.

Let me mingle tears with thee,
Mourning Him who mourned for me,
All the days that I may live.
By the Cross with thee to stay,
There with thee to weep and pray,
Is all I ask of thee to give.

Virgin of all virgins best,
Listen to my fond request:
Let me share thy grief divine.
Let me, to my latest breath,
In my body bear the death
Of that dying Son of thine.

Wounded with His every wound,
Steep my soul till it has swooned
In His very Blood away.
Be to me, O virgin, nigh,
Lest in flames I burn and die,
In His awful Judgment Day.

Christ, when Thou shalt call me hence,
Be Thy Mother my defense,
Be Thy Cross my victory.
While my body here decays,
May my soul Thy goodness praise,
Safe in paradise with Thee. Amen.

LITURGICAL PRAYER

FATHER,
  when Your Son was raised on the cross,
His mother stood by Him, sharing His sufferings.
May Your Church be united with Christ
in His suffering and death
so that it may share in His rising to new life,
where He lives and reigns with You and the
  Holy Spirit,
one God, forever. Amen.

Additional prayers: pp. 198, 208.

Hearken, O daughter, the Lord, thy God, shall greatly desire thy beauty

OCTOBER

OUR LADY OF THE ROSARY

October 7 (Novena: September 28-October 6)

DOCTRINE

ONE of the most highly indulgenced of all devotions, the Rosary is both vocal and mental prayer. Vocally we recite the Our Father, Hail Mary, and Glory Be. Mentally we meditate on the great mysteries of our Faith. The Rosary is a summary of the main events in the life of Jesus and Mary, the Holy Eucharist of the main events in the life of Jesus and Mary. The Holy Eucharist is the testament of Jesus; the Rosary is the testament of Mary. The Joyful Mysteries contain the foundation of the work of our salvation; the Sorrowful, the accomplishing of it; and the Glorious, the perfecting of it. The Popes for nearly four hundred years have recommended the Rosary as the best remedy for the evils afflicting society.

While in the meditation of the mysteries Mary's part in the work of Redemption is considered, in the words of the Hail Mary the lips pay honor to her wonderful dignity and holiness. She is brought before us as the Mediatrix of the graces of the Redemption, the Mother of Mercy, eager to use on behalf of the redeemed a power with God that exceeds that of all other creatures.

The history of the Church bears testimony to the power of the Rosary. For example, the defeat of the Turkish forces which threatened to invade Europe in the naval battle of Lepanto in 1716, and the victories gained over the same enemy in the last century at Temesvar in Hungary are remembered by the establishment of the Feast of Our Lady of Victories by Gregory XIII (1585), which Clement XI (1721) later distinguished by the title of the Holy Rosary.

In our own day Mary has appeared to the children of Fatima in Portugal and proclaimed the pressing need for prayer, especially the Rosary, and sacrifice, if the world is to be saved from the threatening horror of an atheistic way of life. In every age, whether in public or private misfortune, the faithful have turned to Mary.

All Catholics have added to the glory of the Queen of Heaven; and from every corner of this earth has risen the joyous praise of her who is Queen of the Holy Rosary. On earth she was the lowly handmaid of the Lord, and now all generations proclaim the greatness of her name. Obeying the wishes of our Holy Father, Pope Paul VI, in his

Apostolic Exhortation *Marialis Cultus* (February 2, 1974), we should with the simplicity of children turn to Our Lady of the Rosary and endeavor to live a more intense Catholic life.

He wrote: "We wish now, venerable brothers, to dwell for a moment on the renewal of the pious practice which has been called 'the compendium of the entire Gospel,' the Rosary. To this our predecessors have devoted close attention and care. On many occasions they have recommended its frequent recitation, encouraged its diffusion, explained its nature, recognized its suitability for fostering contemplative prayer—prayer of both praise and petition—and recalled its intrinsic effectiveness for promoting Christian life and apostolic commitment" (42).

THE CHURCH SPEAKS

PREDESTINED from eternity—by that decree of divine providence which determined the Incarnation of the Word—to be the Mother of God, the Blessed Virgin was on this earth the Virgin Mother of the Redeemer, and above all others and in a singular way the generous associate and humble handmaid of the Lord. She conceived, brought forth, and nourished Christ, she presented Him to the Father in the Temple, and was united with Him by compassion as He died on the cross. In this singular way she cooperated by her obedience, faith, hope, and burning charity in the work of the Savior in giving back supernatural life to souls. Wherefore she is our Mother in the order of grace.

(Vatican II: *Constitution on the Church*, 61)

Besides her place in the liturgy, our Lady has been honored by an amazingly rich variety of extra-liturgical devotional forms. Some of these have a long history. In particular the Dominican Rosary of 15 decades links our Lady to her Son's salvific career, from the Annunciation and the joyful events of the infancy and childhood of Jesus, through the sorrowful mysteries of His suffering and death, to His Resurrection and Ascension, and the sending of the Spirit to the Apostles at Pentecost, and concluding with the Mother's reunion with her Son in the mysteries of her Assumption and Coronation.

It is unwise to reject the Rosary without a trial simply because of the accusation that it comes from the past, that it is repetitious and ill-suited to sophisticated moderns. The Scriptural riches of the Rosary are of permanent value. Its prayers, in addition to the opening Apostles' Creed and the occasional repetition of the ancient and simple doxology (Glory be to the Father), are the "Our Father" and the "Hail Mary." The words of the first half of the Hail Mary are taken from St. Luke. The second half: "Holy Mary, Mother of God, pray for us sinners, now and at the hour of our death," is in the mainstream of prayers that go back to the early centuries of Christian devotion.

The recommended saying of the Rosary does not consist merely in "telling the beads" by racing through a string of familiar prayers. Interwoven with the prayers are the "mysteries." Almost all of these relate saving events in the life of Jesus, episodes in which the Mother of Jesus shared.

(Behold Your Mother, 96, 97)

PRAYER

MARY, Mother of God, *the joyful mysteries of your Holy Rosary* remind me of the mysteries in which the Word was made flesh and you, the inviolate Virgin and Mother, performed your maternal duties with holy joy. You became the Mother of a Son Who is almighty, eternal, and infinite in all perfections, equal to the Father and to the Holy Spirit. You became the Mother of God without ceasing to be a virgin. By your Divine Motherhood you formed the closest bond of union with the adorable Trinity: the privileged Daughter of the Father, the loving Mother of the Son and the immaculate Bride of the Holy Spirit. By your motherhood you

acquired a mother's power over your Divine
Son, and you saw yourself raised above all the
angels and saints.

The repetition of the Hail Marys keeps
before my mind the importance of the
Incarnation and your share in it. When you
agreed to the proposal made to you by the
angel, you gave Jesus to us by your own free
act. You spoke in behalf of our human nature,
and by your consent sealed forever the union
between our human nature and the Son of
God. Thus, in consenting to the Incarnation,
you cooperated directly in the Redemption of
the world, for the Incarnation was the first step
in the work of our salvation.

Mary, *the sorrowful mysteries of your Holy
Rosary* remind me of the sorrows, the agony,
and death of the suffering Christ, the price, at
which the salvation of our race was accomplished. As Mother of God, you became a
cooperator in the Redemption of mankind. It
was you who prepared the holy Victim Who
was offered to the Eternal Father in expiation
of our sins. From you was derived the Precious
Blood which was shed upon the cross for our
salvation and the adorable Body which, after
having been made the price of our
Redemption, has become the food of our souls
in the Holy Eucharist.

From the moment of His entering the world, your loving Son Jesus was the price of our salvation. He took to Himself our human flesh and became man in order that He might give Himself up for us to the death of the cross. From the very first, He offered Himself as our ransom and the victim for our sins. He did so through your hands when you presented Him in the Temple, and in union with Him you offered yourself to the Father on Calvary.

From the cross Jesus gave you to me to be my Mother, and I was entrusted to your care as your child. You brought me forth spiritually to a new life of grace. This was your spiritual motherhood.

Mary, *the glorious mysteries of the Holy Rosary* remind me of the glory of your Son, Jesus Christ, His triumph over death, His Ascension into heaven, the sending of the Holy Spirit. These mysteries remind me also of your crowning there as Queen of heaven and earth. Finally, they remind me of the everlasting glory of all the saints in heaven united with your own glory and that of your Son. And now as Mother of God and Mother of men, and as Queen of heaven and earth, you serve as a bond between God and men.

As God-Man, Jesus is the perfect Mediator between God and man, because He alone could in all justice merit our reconciliation with God as well as the graces which God would impart after the reconciliation. You are a Mediatrix in union with Christ from Whom your mediation draws all its power. With Christ you have contributed to our Redemption. You consented to be the Mother of the Redeemer at the Annunciation, and thus you were willing to share in the sufferings of the Redeemer. You merited the title CoRedemptrix above all by your union with Christ in His redemptive sacrifice. After Jesus, no one suffered as you did. Now your action is above all one of intercession. In your contemplation of God, you behold our needs with our prayers, and you beg God to grant these favors for us.

May the faithful recitation of my Rosary be a sign of my gratitude to Jesus and to you for all you have done for me in bringing about my Redemption. May the Rosary also be a means of obtaining all the graces I need for the sanctification and salvation of my soul.

HYMN

MOTHER and Maid, the praise of thee
The burden of our song shall be;
Thy joys, thy sorrows, and the crown
Of thine eternal bright renown:

The heavenly tidings brought to earth,
The visitation and the birth,
Christ offered, Christ restored to thee—
Hail, in each Joyful Mystery;

The bloody sweat, the soldier's scorn,
The scourging and the crown of thorn,
The burdened way, the bitter tree—
Hail, in each Woeful Mystery;

The risen and heaven-ascending Lord,
The Pentecostal unction poured,
Thy crown and endless jubilee—
Hail, in each Glorious Mystery.

May age to age forever sing
The Virgin's Son and angel's King,
And praise with the celestial host
The Father, Son, and Holy Ghost.

LITURGICAL PRAYER

LORD, fill our hearts with Your love.
As You revealed to us by an angel
the coming of Your Son as man,
lead us through His suffering and death
to the glory of His resurrection,
Who lives and reigns with You and the Holy
    Spirit,
one God, forever. Amen.

Additional prayer: p. 202.

In the holy dwelling place before **Him** I have ministered

NOVEMBER

PRESENTATION OF MARY

November 21 (Novena: November 12-20)

DOCTRINE

FOR a long time, Mary's parents, Sts. Joachim and Ann, were without children. God rewarded their prayers and granted them a daughter late in life. They may have made a vow before her birth to offer her to God. When Mary was three years old, her parents took her to Jerusalem to present her to God in His Temple.

This event in Mary's childhood was recorded for the first time by St. Evodius, perhaps one of the seventy disciples of our Lord, who was Bishop of Antioch preceding St. Ignatius. St. Jerome, St. Gregory of Nyssa, St. Gregory Nazianzen, and other Church authorities who lived when traditions were still very recent, related the same event and held it as true. Already in the 6th century the event was commemorated in the East. Pope Gregory XI introduced the feast at Avignon and Sixtus V in Rome in 1585 for November 21.

According to apostolic tradition, the writings of the Fathers, and the opinion of the Church, Mary spent her early years in the Temple, that is, from the time of her presentation at the age of three until her espousal to Joseph. The time had come when Mary felt that she could not give herself entirely to God except by the practice of virginity. Divine grace enlightened her that it was the will of God that she make a vow of chastity, even though this was unknown among the Jews.

Under the patronage of our heavenly Mother we should consecrate our whole life to God and serve Him in our state of life with the devotedness and earnestness with which Mary served Him.

THE CHURCH SPEAKS

THE Church in its apostolic work also justly looks to Mary, who, conceived of the Holy Spirit, brought forth Christ, Who was born of the Virgin that through the Church He may be born and may increase in the hearts of the faithful also. The Virgin in her own life lived an example of that maternal love, by which all should be animated who cooperate in the apostolic mission of the Church for the regeneration of men.

(Vatican II: *Constitution on the Church*, 65)

What does "Holy Mary" say to struggling humanity in a sinful world? How does the example of her virtues touch lay men and

women in the pilgrim Church? In her faithful
discipleship, her union with Christ, her open-
ness to the Spirit, Mary stands in contrast to all
the sin, all the evil in the world.

We say "Holy Mary, Mother of God, pray
for us sinners, now and at the hour of our
death," confessing that we have added to the
evil in the world by our own sins, and asking
God's forgiveness. Yet our prayer is filled
with confidence. For we find strength for the
"now" not only in the constant loving intercession of the Mother of God, but also in the
memory of how our Lady of the Gospels lived
the life of faith. The Mother of Jesus is the
great exemplar to the whole Church; but she
is a model also to each individual in the
Church, at every stage of human life and in
every particular Christian vocation. No one
ever followed Jesus so well as Mary His
Mother. No one can help us more, by her
example and by her intercession.

(Behold Your Mother, 129, 130)

PRAYER

MARY, Mother of God, tradition tells us
that when you were three years of age,
*your parents, Joachim and Ann, took you to
the Temple in Jerusalem to fulfill their vow.
They offered you to God by the ministry of
the priest in charge, who invoked the blessing*

of God upon you and your parents. How fervently your mother and father thanked God for having given you to them and begged Him to accept the offering which they were making.

What a beautiful example for parents to imitate! Their children also belong to God, for they are His gift. Teach parents to care for their children as God's sacred trust, to guard them from sin and to lead them in the way of virtue. May they consider it to be the greatest privilege bestowed upon them by God to dedicate their sons and daughters to His holy service.

Mary, *already in your childhood you dedicated yourself to the love and service of God.* Led by divine inspiration to His house, you prepared yourself for your sublime dignity of divine motherhood in silence and solitude with God. You followed with devotion the life led in common by other girls under the care of holy women. When you later returned to your home, you were under the loving care of your mother, St. Ann. With her you loved to recite the psalms and canticles of the inspired authors of your nation. You learned to read the sacred books. You often discussed the coming of the Messiah.

I cannot even imagine the heavenly beauty that adorned your innocent soul as you were prepared by the Eternal Father to be the Mother of His Divine Son and the Bride of the Holy Spirit. The wisdom and power of God was constructing a living temple for the Savior of the world.

Mary, *may the perfect gift of yourself to God through love in your presentation in the Temple be an inspiration to me.* You loved God with your whole heart and mind and strength. Obtain for me the grace to love God with my whole heart, so that all the love my heart is capable of may be consecrated to Him, and all other affection subordinated to the love I owe God.

Help me to love God with my whole soul, so that all the faculties of my soul may be consecrated to Him, and that I may make use of them only to make Him known, loved, and served.

Help me to love God with my whole mind, so that my mind may be habitually occupied with God and that I may value His good pleasure above everything else—above my convenience, knowledge, friendship, health, and even life itself.

Help me to love God with my whole strength, so that I may consecrate undividedly and continually to His service, my life, my health, and all I am and have.

Your first presentation to God, made by the hands of your parents, was an offering most acceptable in His sight. May the consecration of myself to God be made under your patronage and assisted by your intercession and in union with your love and merits.

LITURGICAL PRAYER

ETERNAL Father,
as we honor the holiness and glory of the Virgin Mary,
may her prayers bring us the fullness of Your life and love.
We ask this through our Lord Jesus Christ, Your Son,
one God, forever. Amen.

Additional prayer: p. 200.

Hail, full of grace... Mary,

DECEMBER

THE IMMACULATE CONCEPTION

December 8 (Novena: November 29-December 7)

DOCTRINE

T HE *Immaculate Conception of the Blessed Virgin Mary consists essentially in her exemption from original sin.* From the first moment of her existence her soul was adorned with sanctifying grace which made her a beloved child of God. She was never in that state of separation from God in which all men find themselves before baptism. Mary was preserved from sin in view of the merits of her Son. The grace of the Redeemer prevented her from being tainted by original sin; whereas, we have been rescued from this sin through baptism.

The main reason which demanded the Immaculate Conception for Mary was her divine maternity. It was fitting that the Mother of God be always without sin, even original sin. The *Son of God* could create for Himself a mother most pure; and He certainly has done so. His love for His mother is infinitely greater than ours. If Mary had been conceived in sin, she would have been in a state of enmity toward her Son before He had chosen her as His Mother. Since He had come as Savior to redeem mankind, it was fitting that He redeem His Mother in a more excellent way than the rest of mankind, that is, by preserving her from sin instead of only delivering her from it.

Mary is the privileged daughter of the *Heavenly Father*. He had to make her at least equal to Eve, His first daughter, whom He created immaculate. The *Holy Spirit* made Mary His bride. It was only just that this Spirit of love sanctify her soul in a more sublime manner than all other souls by preventing sin from entering, instead of merely driving it out.

The Immaculate Conception entails a great number of *heavenly favors*. With her original grace Mary received the principal gifts which God gave Adam for the perfection of his nature—gifts which are not restored to us with the grace of baptism. In Mary there were no unruly desires of the flesh, no moral or religious ignorance that would have caused disorder, no weakness in the will, no bodily infirmities. Her sufferings were sufferings of love— love for her Son and for us. Like Him, she was also to die, but her death was an ecstasy of love.

The Fathers, the early writers of the Church, believed that Mary was free from sin in her conception. In 1453 the Immaculate Conception was defined as a pious belief, in harmony with the devotion of the Church, reason, and Holy Scripture. On December 8, 1854, Pope Pius IX solemnly promulgated the dogma in these words: "We pronounce and define that the doctrine which states that the Most Blessed Virgin Mary was in the first instant of her conception, by the singular grace and privilege of God, in view of the merits of Jesus Christ, the Savior of the human race, preserved immune from all stain of original sin, has been revealed by God and is therefore to be firmly and unswervingly believed by all the faithful."

Devotion to Mary Immaculate will lead us to imitate the sinlessness of the Blessed Virgin Mary and her perfect love for Jesus. We should take the Immaculate Virgin as the special protectress of the purity of our body and soul.

The United States was dedicated to the Immaculate Conception by the Third Plenary Council of Baltimore in 1846.

THE CHURCH SPEAKS

SINCE it has pleased God not to manifest solemnly the mystery of the salvation of the human race before He would pour forth the Spirit promised by Christ, we see the apostles before the day of Pentecost "persevering with one mind in prayer with the women and Mary the Mother of Jesus, and with His brethren," and Mary by her prayers imploring the gift of the Spirit, Who had already overshadowed her in the Annunciation. Finally, the Immaculate Virgin, preserved free from all guilt of original sin, on the completion of her earthly sojourn, was taken up body and soul into heavenly glory, and exalted by the Lord as Queen of the universe, that she might be the more fully conformed to her Son, the Lord of lords and the conqueror of sin and death.

(Vatican II: *Constitution on the Church*, 59)

The Virgin Mary was called by the Fathers of the Church "all holy," the term beloved to this day by Christians in the East. She was declared to be "free from all stain of sin," "fashioned by the Holy Spirit into a kind of new substance and a new creature." The Second Vatican Council asserts that she was "adorned with the radiance of a singular holiness from the first moment of her conception. . . ." In this statement, the Council calls attention to the doctrine of the Immaculate Conception. In 1854 Pope Pius IX defined as revealed truth "that the Blessed Virgin Mary in the first instant of her conception, by a singular grace and privilege of almighty God, in view of the foreseen merits of Jesus Christ the Savior of the human race, was preserved free from all stain of original sin."

(*Behold Your Mother*, 52)

PRAYER

MARY, *Mother of God, I believe what Holy Mother Church teaches about your Immaculate Conception:* that from the first moment of your conception you possessed justice and holiness—that is, sanctifying grace, even the fullness of grace, with the infused virtues and gifts of the Holy Spirit, and with integrity of nature; yet you remained subject to death and other pains and miseries of life that your Son Himself willed to undergo.

For the first time after thousands of years God, in His wisdom and power and love, created again a human being in that state in which He had created our first parents. Immaculate Virgin, you are that human being. Because of sanctifying grace infused into your soul, you were from the first moment of your existence most intimately united with God and endowed with the most precious gifts of heaven. You possessed a perfect faith, a firm hope, a burning love, a deep humility, a purity greater than that of the angels.

Your soul is the creation and the masterpiece of almighty workmanship. The Angel Gabriel said: "Hail, full of grace"—there was no room for sin; "the Lord is with you"—where God dwells, Satan can have no rights; "blessed are you among women"—you were elevated above all other women in the world.

Mary, Mother of God, no stain of original sin ever defiled your pure soul. *This privilege separated you from all the rest of the children of Adam.* As the Mother of the Incarnate Son you were so preserved from inheriting original sin that never for a moment was so much as a shadow cast by sin upon your spotless soul. You were the only one who was exempt from the universal curse that had fallen on the whole human race. You were never under the power of the serpent, whose head you crushed in giving a Redeemer to the world. Your Immaculate Conception is a triumph over Satan, the author of evil, who, under your heel, suffered his first complete defeat. It is but a symbol of the endless victories which you are to win over him to the last day.

But you needed the redeeming Savior to obtain this exemption, deliverance from the universal debt of being subject to original sin. Being the new Eve who was to be the Mother of the new Adam, you were, by the eternal decree of God and by the merits of Christ, withdrawn from the general law of original sin. Your redemption was the very masterpiece of Christ's redeeming wisdom. He paid the debt that original sin might not be incurred.

Mary, Mother of God, *your greatness began at the first instant of your existence with the privilege of your Immaculate Conception.* After Almighty God and the Sacred Humanity of Jesus, there is no being so great as you. It is true, you are a creature, and, therefore, far beneath the Supreme Being. But you are a creature so holy and so perfect that you are superior to all other creatures.

It was fitting that you, a Virgin Mother, should conceive the Man Who was also the Son of God. It was fitting that you should be adorned with the greatest purity ever possible to a creature. You are the Virgin to whom God the Father decreed to give His only Son —the Divine Word, equal with Himself in all things—that entering the natural order He might become your Son as well as His. You are the immaculate Virgin whom the Son Himself chose to make His Mother. You are the immaculate Virgin whom the Holy Spirit willed to make His bride and in whom He would work the tremendous miracle of the Incarnation. The privilege of the Immaculate Conception. was suitable to your dignity.

Mary, my Mother, help me to imitate your sinlessness by keeping my soul free from every willful sin by the faithful observance of God's commandments. Help me to imitate your fullness of grace by receiving Holy Communion frequently, where I shall obtain the sanctifying grace that will make my soul holy and pleasing to God, and the actual graces I need to practice virtue. Through prayer may grace fill my soul with the life of God and transform me into a living image of Jesus, just as you were.

LITURGICAL PRAYER

FATHER, You prepared the Virgin Mary
 to be the worthy Mother of Your Son.
You made it possible for her to share beforehand
in the salvation Your Son, Jesus Christ,
would bring by His death,
and kept her without sin from the first moment of her conception.
Give us the grace by her prayers
ever to live in Your presence without sin.
We ask this through the same Christ, our Lord.
  Amen.

Additional prayer: p. 194.

OUR LADY
OF
GUADALUPE

December 12 (Triduum:
December 9-11)

DOCTRINE

ACCORDING to tradition the Blessed Virgin appeared to a fifty-five-year-old Aztec Indian named Juan Diego, who was hurrying to hear Mass in Mexico City, on Saturday, December 9, 1531. She sent him to Bishop Zumarraga to ask that a Church be built on the spot where she stood. She was at the same place that evening and Sunday evening to get the bishop's answer. After cross-questioning Juan, the bishop ordered him to ask for a sign from the lady who had said she was the Mother of God.

Juan was occupied all Monday with Bernardino, an uncle, who seemed dying of fever. On Tuesday, December 12th, the grieved nephew had to run for a priest and, to avoid the apparition, slipped around where the chapel now stands. But the Blessed Virgin came to meet him and said that she had cured his uncle and asked him to go again to the bishop. He asked for a sign. She told him to go up to the rocks and gather roses. He knew it was neither the time nor the place for roses, but he obeyed.

Gathering the roses into the long cloak worn by Mexican Indians, he returned to the Blessed Mother, who arranged them and warned him to keep them unseen till he reached the bishop. When he arrived at the bishop's home, Juan unfolded his cloak and the roses fell out. Startled to see the bishop and his attendants kneeling before him, he looked at the cloak and saw there the life-sized figure of the Virgin Mother, just as he had described her. The picture was venerated in the bishop's chapel and soon after carried in procession to the first shrine.

The picture which has aroused all this devotion is a representation of the Immaculate Conception, with the sun, moon, and stars, according to the text in the Book of Revelation. Mary clothed in a blue robe dotted with stars, stands on the crescent moon. Underneath the crescent is a support angel. The rays of the sun shoot out on all sides from behind the central figure.

The coarsely woven material which bears the picture is as thin and open as poor sacking. It is made of vegetable fiber and consists of two strips, about seventy inches long by eighteen wide, held together by weak stitching. The chief colors imprinted on this material are deep gold in the rays and stars, blue-green in the mantle, and rose in the flowered tunic.

In 1709 a rich shrine was erected; in 1904 it was made a basilica. Guadalupe, in the Aztec Indian tongue, means "She shall crush your head," but has been extended to the church containing the picture and to the town that grew up around it, which is three miles northeast of Mexico City, Mexico. Pilgrimages have been made to this shrine almost uninterruptedly since 1531. Twenty Popes favored the shrine and its tradition. Pope Pius X decreed that Our Lady of Guadalupe should be the national patron, and made December 12th a holyday of obligation.

When Our Lady imprinted her image on the cloak of Juan Diego, there was no United States. From the Gulf to the St. Lawrence was one continent, and that continent had been dedicated to Our Lady by the Spaniards. The United States was dedicated to the Immaculate Conception by the Third Plenary Council of Baltimore in 1846. The Image of Our Lady of Guadalupe is the image of the Immaculate Conception. She is the Woman of the Book of Revelation, clothed with the sun, standing on the moon, and, though without the crown of stars, wears them on her mantle. Significantly, the Child Jesus does not appear.

The apparition of our Lady of Guadalupe is Mary's only recorded appearance in North America. Pope Pius XII said, "We are certain that so long as you—Our Lady of Guadalupe—are recognized as Queen and Mother, America and Mexico are saved." He proclaimed her the Patroness of the Americas. As patroness of Pan-American unity, Our Lady of Guadalupe influences her children to turn toward one another in common love for her and her beloved Son.

THE CHURCH SPEAKS

THERE is but one Mediator as we know from the words of the apostles, "for there is one God and one mediator of God and men, the man Christ Jesus, Who gave Himself as a redemption for all." The maternal duty of Mary toward men in no wise obscures or diminishes this unique mediation of Christ, but rather shows His power.

For all the salvific influence of the Blessed Virgin on men originates, not from some inner necessity, but from the divine pleasure. It flows forth from the superabundance of the merits of Christ, rests on His mediation, depends entirely on it and draws all its power from it. In no way does it impede, but rather it fosters the immediate union of the faithful with Christ.

(Vatican II: *Constitution on the Church*, 60)

Mary's initial holiness, a totally unmerited gift of God, is a sign of the love of Christ for His Bride the Church, which, though composed of sinners, is still "holy Church." Mary Immaculate is seen in relation to Christ and the Church. Her privileged origin is the final step in preparing mankind to receive the Redeemer. God's grace triumphed over the power of original sin; the Father chose a perfectly responsive mother for the incarnate Son. The grace of the Immaculate Conception, a charism totally from God, prepared Mary for the motherhood of Jesus, the Savior. The Virgin Mary is "the most excellent fruit of the redemption," a figure of the spotless bride of Christ, which is the Church.

(Behold Your Mother, 56)

PRAYER

MARY, Mother of God, *in honoring you as Our Lady of Guadalupe, we honor you as the Immaculate Conception.* The picture you imprinted on the cloak of the Indian at Guadalupe was the image of the Immaculate Conception. You appeared as the Woman of the Apocalypse, clothed with the sun, standing on the moon.

I believe the doctrine of the Church concerning your Immaculate Conception, which teaches that at the first moment of your conception you were, by the singular grace and privilege of the omnipotent God, in virtue of the merits of Jesus Christ, Savior of the human race, preserved from all stain of original sin.

The foundation of this doctrine is to be found in Sacred Scripture where we are taught that God, the Creator of all things, after the sad fall of Adam, addressed the serpent in words which the Church applies to you: "I will put enmity between you and the woman, and between your offspring and hers; he will strike at your head, while you strike at his heal" (Gen 3:15). If at any time you had been without divine grace, even for the shortest moment, there would not have come between you and the serpent that everlasting enmity spoken of by God.

Since in the Bible you are called "full of grace" and "blessed among women," your soul was the abode of divine grace, adorned with the Gifts of the Holy Spirit, so that you were never subjected to the evil spirit.

May the example of your sinlessness urge us to that innocence and purity of life which flees from and abhors even the slightest stain of sin. Forming with your Divine Son one spiritual body, we experience the rage of Satan until the end of time. But we, too, by our union with Jesus, and by the power of His grace, will also be united with Him in His victory over the devil.

Mary, your apparition at Guadalupe teaches me that *devotion to you is a source of great graces*. The Church has always taught that God has entrusted to your hands heavenly blessings. I have but to ask for them for the salvation of my soul. There is nothing you want more than to give them to me, because you are even more anxious to save my soul than I am, for you know better than anyone else the price your Son paid for it and the precious worth of each grace He so graciously offers to me through you.

Devotion to you brings with it consolation for the soul. As a child runs to its mother in every need, and finds comfort in her glance and kind word, I can turn to you for help when I need it, for you are truly my Mother, whose heart is overflowing with kindness and mercy.

Mary, *your apparition at Guadalupe as the Immaculate Conception is your only recorded appearance in North America.* Bless the people of the Americas, to which uncounted thousands have come to seek refuge and livelihood. Preserve their faith, assailed by the forces opposed to Christ. Petition God that their hope may never fail amid the troubles and the cares of this life. We beg you for a burning charity for God to imitate the works of Christ. We ask you to procure for us, by your prayers, the great grace of final perseverance so that those who are joined to honor you in the kingdom of your Son on earth may be together always in heaven.

HYMN

SIGN of Salvation with Jesus the Light,
Clothed with the Sun thou art radiant bright!
Promised of old as the serpent's defeat,
Queenly adored with the moon 'neath thy feet!

Garden of Eden, where sin has no part,
Life-giving Tree, bearing Christ in your heart.
Ark, where the Manna was hidden away,
Holy of Holies, Immaculate Way!

City of God, with the Lamb as thy Light,
Dawn of Eternal Day knowing no night!
Bride of the Spirit and Mother of God,
Heavenly Path which the blessed trod!

OUR Lady of Guadalupe, mystical rose,
make intercession for holy Church,
protect the Sovereign Pontiff,
help all those who invoke you in their needs,
and since you are the ever Virgin Mary
and Mother of the true God,
obtain for us from your most holy Son
the grace of keeping our faith,
sweet hope in the midst of the bitterness of life,
burning charity and the precious gift of final perseverance. Amen.

LITURGICAL PRAYER

GOD of power and mercy,
You blessed the Americas at Tepeyac
with the apparition of the Virgin Mary of
   Guadalupe.
May her prayers help all men and women
to accept each other as brothers and sisters.
Through your justice present in our hearts
may Your peace reign in the world.

We ask this through our Lord Jesus Christ,
  Your Son,
Who lives and reigns with You and the Holy
  Spirit,
one God, forever. Amen.

Additional prayer: p. 192.

From the stump
of Jesse
a bud
will blossom

NATIVITY OF OUR LORD

December 25 (Octave prayers till January 1)

DOCTRINE

AFTER her visit of three months to Elizabeth, Mary returned to Nazareth. Joseph had not as yet been informed of the angel's visit to Mary. Seeing that she was to become a mother, and not wishing to accuse her, for he was "an upright man" and could not question her virtue, he decided to send her away secretly. An angel appeared to him in a dream and said, "Joseph, son of David, do not be afraid to receive Mary into your home as your wife. For this child has been conceived in her womb through the Holy Spirit" (Mt 1:20). Joseph did as the Lord had commanded: he took his spouse to his home.

Emperor Augustus ordered that a census be taken. Since all had to enroll in their home town, Joseph went up from Nazareth in Galilee to the city of David in Judea, called Bethlehem, because he was of the house and family of David; he went up with Mary, his espoused wife, who was with child. The trip took about four days. Because of the many travelers, there was no room for them in the inn. They found shelter in a stable, where Mary brought into the world her firstborn Son, wrapped Him in swaddling clothes, and laid Him in a manger. She adored her little Son Who was also her God. An angel informed the shepherds of the birth of a Savior, and they hastened to adore Him also. Mary kept these things, pondering over them in her heart. It is to her that we owe the details concerning the birth and childhood of Jesus.

Especially in the Incarnation and Redemption God's infinite goodness and mercy shine forth. His eternal plan of sending His own Son into the world to redeem the human race, broken and bruised by sin, and of restoring to it the children's inheritance and heavenly beatitude, is the masterpiece of His wisdom and love. The Blessed Virgin Mary had a very important part in this eternal plan as the Mother of the Redeemer.

Christmas recalls the wonderful mystery of the Incarnation which renders God visible in order that we may listen to Him, imitate Him and unite ourselves to Him. It renders God able to suffer, for He finds in His humanity the means wherewith to suffer, to expiate, to merit, to enrich us with graces. The Word of God assumed our human nature to redeem us and to make us holy by giving us a share in His divinity. It was through the Virgin Mary that Jesus received His humanity; hence the feast of Christmas belongs both to Christ and to His Blessed Mother. The gift of Christ was perfectly accomplished at the moment of His birth. Just as there can never be a Christmas without Christ, so there can never be a Christ without a Mary.

Holy Church wishes that the celebration of the mystery of our Lord's Incarnation should bring us the grace that we may live a new life, more free from sin and attachment to ourselves and creatures. She would have us understand above all that Christ, in exchange for His humanity which He takes from us, wishes to make us partakers of His divinity by sanctifying grace, that He may possess us completely. The grace of His new divine birth in us is the true meaning and spirit of Christmas. Just as our Blessed Mother had an intimate share in giving Jesus to us, she also has an intimate share in obtaining the graces of Christmas for us.

THE CHURCH SPEAKS

THIS union of the Mother with the Son in the work of salvation is made manifest from the time of Christ's virginal conception up to His death. It is shown first of all when Mary, arising in haste to go to visit Elizabeth, is greeted by her as blessed because of her belief in the promise of salvation and the precursor leaped with joy in the womb of his mother. This union is manifest also at the birth of Our Lord, Who did not diminish His mother's virginal integrity but sanctified it, when the Mother of God joyfully showed her firstborn Son to the shepherds and Magi.

(Vatican II: *Constitution on the Church*, 57)

It was prophesied in the Old Testament that the Spirit would revivify all things, would create a new people, renew the face of the earth. The overshadowing Spirit Who brings about the virginal conception of the Son of Mary is the same powerful Spirit. The Virgin birth is not simply a privilege affecting only Jesus and Mary, but a sign and means for the Spirit to build the new People of God, the Body of Christ, the Church. The glorious positive sign value of the Virgin birth is the merciful and free saving grace of the Father sending His Son, conceived by the Holy Spirit, born of the Virgin Mary, that we might receive the adoption of sons.

(Behold Your Mother, 48)

PRAYER

MARY, Mother of God, *how wondrous was the birth of your Divine Son!* To fulfill the prophecy that the Messiah would be born in Bethlehem, the city of David, God made use of the edict of a pagan emperor. With Joseph you went up from Galilee into Judea, to Bethlehem, the city of David, because you were of the house and family of David, to be enrolled. In your delicate condition, in winter, and without even the necessities of life for yourself or your child, you obediently traveled to a distant and strange land. You did not question the plans of God but hastened to fulfill them, for your confidence in God matched your love of Him.

You conceived Him by the Holy Spirit with all purity, and with all purity you brought Him forth, not in the pangs of childbirth but in the happiness of yearning love. In a poor cave of Bethlehem the Son of God was born miraculously. His human soul and body were substantially and inseparably united to His divine nature in one Divine Person, being the soul and body of God Incarnate. Through this birth, the Divine Majesty lost nothing of Its splendor, and you became the Mother of God and yet remained a virgin.

This mystery and your dignity amaze heaven and earth. Never had God Himself submitted to man, and He submitted to you. Never had God consulted man, and He consulted you. Never had God made His actions depend on man, and He made the most wonderful of His actions depend on you! From the moment you pronounced the words, "I am the servant of the Lord. Let it be done to me according to your word," God dwelt bodily within you. The angels adored this mystery of the abasement of the Son of God, as well as His compassion and love for men, and rejoiced in your dignity, greatness, power, for you are truly His Mother.

I can picture you lovingly embracing your little Son and adoring Him as your God; wrapping Him in swaddling clothes and gently laying Him on the straw in the manger. There were only two spectators to witness the birth of God's own Son. Only your deep faith could fully appreciate this extreme poverty. The God of infinite power was now a helpless Infant, subject to the suffering of frail mortals. You adored the God Whom the heavens could not contain, cribbed and confined in the narrow manger.

Mary, I cannot even imagine *the joy that filled your heart as you gazed at your Child* with wondering awe, lifted Him from the manger, cradled Him in your arms and pressed Him to your heart. The love that welled up in His little heart was divine love, and you must have received it with the utmost humility, never for a moment deeming yourself worthy of it, but returning the favor with all the love of your own immaculate heart.

Such love set your heart on fire with love of your Infant Son; not merely as your Son, but as your God and Savior, since you have already shared in the merits of His Passion and death. You loved Him according to the measure of the grace with which you were full. I have but a very faint notion of the delight that overflowed your soul as a result of such love.

The love of your Divine Child, which was the reason for your great joy, was also the cause of your sorrow. You knew that this little Son of yours was God's Son and that God had not given Him to you for yourself alone, but for the whole world. That little Infant in the manger was your own flesh and blood. Someday you would give that life of Jesus as a sacrifice for the salvation of the world. You received both joy and sorrow with perfect resignation to the divine will.

Mary, *how great was your love for Jesus!* When the little Jesus was not yet born, from the depths of your humble soul you sent your prayers to Him. When men's heartlessness thrust Jesus and you from Bethlehem to the cold stable, your arms warmed the Savior. When Herod's cruelty drove you into the Egyptian desert, your virginal breast was the only safe resting place for your little Son. When Jesus began to develop, your pure eyes guarded Him day and night. And when He struggled with death on Calvary, then again it was you, His Mother. who stood faithfully at the foot of the cross with the sword of pain piercing your heart.

Like you, help me to strive with every power within me to love Jesus for His own sake. May that love impress itself on all my thoughts, words, and actions. Like you, let me willingly

accept and bear the cross in the spirit of a true
follower of my crucified Master.

Your soul was stirred with sentiments of
admiration for the wondrous providence of
God when you saw the first adorers of your
Divine Child who had been led to the crib by
the message of an angel. You fully appreciated
the meaning of your own poverty and kept all
these things, pondering them in your heart.
Help me to learn the lesson of humility, poverty, and self-denial which Jesus preached from
His first pulpit, the little crib.

HYMN

THE Holy Spirit chose thee for His Bride,
   His favored Spouse immaculate to be.
By Him thy soul was made and beautified,
A spotless temple for the Trinity.
What veiled magnificence in thee I see:
No earthly pomp and fleeting greatness thine,
But from all stain of sin thy soul is free,
And bright within thy countless virtues shine,
For in thy heart there reigns a Spouse Who is divine.

Within the realms of God's thought,
Thou wast ordained the hope of paradise.
And in thy soul the Holy Spirit brought
The splendor which devotion glorifies.
He made thee pure and spotless in His eyes,
A spouse like to no other spouse on earth;
Salvation's Sun from thee could nobly rise,
O Queen of Saints, before thy blessed birth!
What feeble mortal tongue can fully praise thy
   worth!

O gentle Queen, the Spirit's chaste abode,
Help us prepare for Him a worthy throne.
The way is dark and life a weary road;
Our will is weak, 'neath sorrow's sting we groan.
To thee we turn in exile and alone,
To see His presence singing in thy heart.
Our consecration to His love we own;
As thou thyself His tabernacle art,
His temples we shall be, and ne'er from Him depart.

LITURGICAL PRAYER

GOD of love, Father of all,
the darkness that covered the earth
has given way to the bright dawn
of Your Word made flesh.
Make us a people of this light.
Make us faithful to Your Word,
that we may bring Your life to the waiting
world.
Grant this through Christ our Lord. Amen.

Additional prayers: pp. 191, 207.

HOLY FAMILY

Sunday in the Octave of Christmas

DOCTRINE

ALL that the Gospels tell us of *Christ's hidden life at Nazareth* with Mary and Joseph is that He "was obedient to them," and that Jesus, for His part, "increased in wisdom and in age and in grace with God and men" (Lk 2:52). Jesus could say of His Mother and foster father what he said of His heavenly Father, "I do always the things that please them." Out of a life of thirty-three years, Jesus, Who is Eternal Wisdom, chose to pass thirty years in silence and obscurity, obedience and labor. Truly, He is a hidden God! It was in this hidden life at Nazareth that Mary had the rare privilege of observing the example of her divine Son and of becoming more like Him in grace and virtue.

The Holy Family is a model for all Christian families. In the family life of Jesus, Mary, and Joseph are exemplified the proper relations that should exist between husband and wife, parents and children. There was filial devotion to God in that family circle

of the three holiest persons who ever lived. While
Joseph supported the Holy Family by handwork,
Mary managed the household, and Jesus assisted
both of them. They were united in their daily tasks
which they made holy by prayer and meditation. By
practicing the domestic virtues of charity, obedience,
and mutual help, they sanctified family life. We
should often pray to them to sanctify our families by
their example and intercession.

THE CHURCH SPEAKS

THE perfect example of this type of spiritual and apostolic life is the most Blessed
Virgin Mary, Queen of Apostles, who while
leading the life common to all here on earth,
one filled with family concerns and labors, was
always intimately united with her Son and in
an entirely unique way cooperated in the work
of the Savior. Having now been assumed into
heaven, with her maternal charity she cares for
these brothers of her Son who are still on their
earthly pilgrimage and remain involved in
dangers and difficulties until they are lead into
the happy homeland. All should devoutly venerate her and commend their life and apostolate to her maternal care.

(Vatican II: *Decree on Apostolate of the Laity*, 49)

What does Mary mean to today's family?
Mother of the Holy Family at Nazareth, Mary
is mother and queen of every Christian family.

When Mary conceived and gave birth to Jesus, human motherhood reached its greatest achievement. From the time of the Annunciation, she was the living chalice of the Son of God made man. In the tradition of her people she recognized that God gives life and watches over its growth. "Just as you do not know the way of the wind or the mysteries of a woman with child, no more do you know the work of God Who is behind it all" (Eccl 11:5).

God called Mary and Joseph to sublimate the consummation of their married love in exclusive dedication to the Holy Child, conceived not by a human father but by the Holy Spirit. When Mary said to Gabriel, "How can this be since I do not know man?" (Lk 1:34), the angel told her of the virginal conception. Joseph received the same message in a dream. Christian tradition from early times has seen Saint Joseph as protector of the Christ Child and of his wife's consecrated virginity throughout their married life.

Mary is Queen of the home. As a woman of faith, she inspires all mothers to transmit the Christian faith to their children. In the setting of family love, children should learn free and loving obedience, inspired by Mary's obedience to God.

(Behold your Mother, 131, 133, 137)

PRAYER

MARY, Mother of God, *how wonderful and yet at times how painful were the experiences of your hidden life with Jesus!* After the Annunciation, the most joyful experience of your life was *the birth of Jesus* at Bethlehem. With all purity you had conceived Him, with all purity you had brought Him forth in the bliss of love. You adored and loved Him in the company of Joseph. Later, encouraged by your smile, poor shepherds drew near to the crib to pay homage to your newly born Son. And when they told you about the message of the angel, you kept these things, pondering over them in your heart.

On the eighth day you were present at the *circumcision* of your Child when He was given the name Jesus. This name, meaning Savior, must have recalled for you the mission for which Jesus had willed to be born of you. With what love you and Joseph pronounced this most charming of all names, when you addressed the Son of God.

On the fortieth day you and Joseph brought the Child to Jerusalem *to present Him to the Lord* according to the law of Moses. Who will understand the anguish of your heart when Simeon reminded you that your gentle Child, Who was to bring salvation and peace to men, would be an occasion for the fall even of many of His brethren in Israel and that your heart would be pierced by a sword of sorrow? Henceforth there would hardly be an hour of joy unmixed with sadness for you.

But what happiness filled your heart when you witnessed the adoration of your Child by the three learned *kings of the East* as they narrated to you, with beautiful simplicity, their account of the mysterious star that had led them to Christ! Having adored their God, they paid reverence to you, His Mother, but you referred their homage to your Son, with Whom you were one in the redemption of souls. You were grateful to God for having revealed Him to the pagan nations of the world.

Your faith was severely tried by the command of the angel *to flee into Egypt*. Your Son was the Son of the Most High; yet you, His Mother, had to defend Him, the King of kings, from the hatred of an earthly king by flight into a pagan land. You obeyed at once and started in the darkness of the night on your long journey with your divine Child and Joseph. Though your stay in this land must have been very unpleasant, you awaited a sign from heaven before returning to your own country.

Words cannot describe the sorrow of your motherly heart when *you lost your twelve-*

year-old Son. You expressed your grief in the gentle complaint, "Son, why have You done this to us? Your father and I have been searching for You with great anxiety" (Lk 2:48). After doing what He regarded as His Father's will, Jesus went down with you and Joseph and came to Nazareth and was obedient to you.

Help me to learn from your hidden life with Jesus, that no matter how heavy my cross, I have nothing to fear as long as God is with me. Teach me to surrender myself to the divine will with the childlike confidence which you had in the Providence of God.

Mary, your life at Nazareth was *a hidden life of prayer and work*. Your whole day's work was done for God alone because prayer, simple and sublime, filled it completely. A charming simplicity dominated each of your domestic duties. Your disposition was always serene because the thought of God absorbed you. Your heart was in your home. You were satisfied with only the necessities of life. Sanctity was carefully concealed beneath the quiet simplicity of your daily life so that people did not realize the Son of God and his Virgin Mother dwelt among them.

How reverently you and Joseph admired the beautiful example of Jesus! His practice of obedience gave to the hidden life of Nazareth its sweetness, peace, and majesty. Though He was the Son of God, He was subject to His creatures for thirty years. We cannot measure your growth in holiness. Grace poured constantly from Christ, its source, into your soul, and you were the channel through which it was imparted to his foster father. While your hands were busy, Jesus absorbed your thoughts and affections and thrilled your hearts with the purest love for Him. Divine love united you all in a holy and happy family.

Mary, *the imitation of your Divine Son was the great occupation of your life.* It thrilled you with the purest joy to have so perfect a Model ever before you; to talk freely and often with Him; to be so close an observer of His conduct. You filled your mind unceasingly with thoughts of His virtues. You pondered over all His words and recorded them in your heart. You were absorbed in acquiring His spirit. You spent yourself and were spent in learning the practical knowledge of Jesus Christ, and in so doing, you became the holiest creature that ever walked this earth.

If I am to be a child worthy of so wonderful a Mother, I must burn with the same desire to imitate Him. Help me to study my Divine Model with earnestness and perseverance, as you did and thus gain the knowledge that will be for me eternal life.

Help me to copy your example and to see in a hidden life of prayer, work, and daily fidelity to the commonplace, the surest steppingstone to a holy life. Like you, may I with reverent familiarity speak to my God and ask Him to enlighten me about His providence in my regard and strengthen me to bear the crosses He sends me.

HYMN

O HIGHEST Hope of mortals,
Blest Light of saints above,
O Jesus, on whose boyhood
Home smiled with kindly love.

And thou whose bosom nursed Him,
O Mary, highly graced,
Whose breast gave milk to Jesus,
Whose arms thy God embraced.

And thou of all men chosen
To guard the Virgin's fame,
to whom God's Son refused not
a father's gracious name.

Born for the nation's healing,
Of Jesse's lineage high,
Behold the supplicants kneeling,
O hear the sinners' cry!

The sun, returned to evening,
Dusks all the twilight air:
We, lingering here before You,
Pour out our heartfelt prayer.

Your home was a garden
Made glad with fairest flowers;
May life thus blossom sweetly
In every home of ours.

Jesus, to Thee be glory
The Maiden-Mother's Son,
With Father and with Spirit
While endless ages run.

LITURGICAL PRAYER

FATHER,
help us to live like the holy family,
united in respect and love.
We ask You to bring us
to the joy and peace of Your eternal home.
Grant this through our Lord Jesus Christ, Your
   Son,
Who lives and reigns with You and the Holy
   Spirit,
one God, forever. Amen.

Additional prayer: p. 210.

"You are the great honor of our people."

Part 2

PRAYERS
OF THE SAINTS
TO OUR LADY

PRAYERS OF THE SAINTS TO OUR LADY

Mary, Vessel of God's Mysteries

MARY, you are the vessel and tabernacle containing all mysteries. You know what the Patriarchs never knew; you have experienced what was never revealed to the Angels; you have heard what the Prophets never heard. In a word, all that was hidden from preceding generations was made known to you; even more, most of these wonders depended on you.

—St Gregory Thaumaturgus († 270)

Mary, Our Hope

BLESSED Virgin, immaculate and pure, you are the sinless Mother of your Son, the mighty Lord of the universe. You are holy and inviolate, the hope of the hopeless and sinful; we sing your praises. We praise you as full of every grace, for you bore the God-Man. We all venerate you; we invoke you and implore your aid.

Holy and immaculate Virgin, rescue us from every need that presses upon us and from all the temptations of the devil. Be our intercessor and advocate at the hour of death and judgment. Deliver us from the fire that is not extinguished and from the outer darkness.

Make us worthy of the glory of your Son, O dearest and most kind Virgin Mother. You indeed are our most secure and only hope for you are holy in the sight of God, to Whom be honor and glory, majesty, and power forever.

—St. Ephrem of Edessa († 373)

Mary, Mother of Grace

IT BECOMES you to be mindful of us, as you stand near Him Who granted you all graces, for you are the Mother of God and our Queen. Help us for the sake of the King, the Lord God Master Who was born of you. For this reason you are called "full of grace."

Remember us, most holy Virgin, and bestow on us gifts from the riches of your graces, Virgin, full of grace.

—St. Athanasius († 373)

Mary, Mother of Mercy

BLESSED Virgin Mary, who can worthily repay you with praise and thanksgiving for having rescued a fallen world by your generous consent? What songs of praises can our weak human nature offer in your honor, since it was through you that it has found the way to salvation? Accept then such poor thanks as we have to offer, unequal though they be to your merits. Receive our gratitude and obtain by your prayers the pardon of our sins. Take our prayers into the sanctuary of heaven and enable them to bring about our peace with God.

May the sins we penitently bring before Almighty God through you be pardoned. May what we beg with confidence be granted through you. Take our offering and grant our request; obtain pardon for what we fear, for you are the only hope of sinners. We hope to obtain the forgiveness of our sins through you. Blessed Lady, in you is our hope of reward.

Holy Mary, help the miserable, strengthen the discouraged, comfort the sorrowful, pray for your people, plead for the clergy, intercede for all women consecrated to God. May all who venerate you, feel now your help and protection. Be ready to help us when we pray, and bring back to us the answers to our prayers. Make it your continual care to pray for the people of God, for you were blessed by God and were made worthy to bear the Redeemer of the world, Who lives and reigns forever.

—St. Augustine († 430)

Mary, Mother and Virgin

HAIL, Mother and Virgin, imperishable Temple of the Godhead, venerable treasure of the whole world, crown of virginity, support of the true faith upon which the Church is founded throughout the whole world.

Mother of God, you enclosed under your heart the infinite God, Whom no space can contain. Through you the Most Holy Trinity is adored and glorified, demons are banished, and our fallen nature again assumed into heaven. Through you the human race, held captive in the bonds of idolatry, arrives at the knowledge of truth.

Hail, through whom kings rule, through whom the only-begotten Son of God has become a star of light to those who were sitting in darkness and in the shadow of death!

—St. Cyril of Alexandria († 444)

Mary, Life of Christians

WHO could know God, were it not for you, most holy Mary? Who could be saved? Who would be preserved from dangers? Who would receive any grace, were it not for you, Mother of God, full of grace? What hope could we have of salvation, if you abandon us, O Mary, who are the life of Christians?

—St. Germanus of Constantinople († 732)

Mary, Hope of Christians

HAIL Mary, hope of Christians, hear the prayer of a sinner who loves you tenderly, who honors you in a special manner, who places in you the hope of his salvation. I owe you my life.

You obtain for me the grace of your Divine Son. You are the sure pledge of my eternal happiness. I entreat you, deliver me from the burden of my sins, take away the darkness of my mind, destroy the earthly affections of my heart, defeat the temptations of my enemies, and rule all the actions of my life so that with you as guide I may arrive at the eternal happiness of heaven.

—St. John Damascene († 754)

Mary, Beloved of the Trinity

HOLY Virgin Mary, there is none like you among women born in the world. Daughter and handmaid of the heavenly Father, the Almighty King. Mother of our Most High Lord Jesus Christ! Spouse of the Holy Spirit! Pray for us to your most holy Son, our Lord and Master.

Hail, holy Lady, most noble Queen, Mother of God, Mary ever Virgin! You were chosen by the heavenly Father, who has been pleased to honor you with the presence of His most holy Son and Divine Paraclete. You were blessed with the fullness of grace and goodness.

Hail, Temple of God, His dwelling-place, His masterpiece, His handmaid. Hail, Mother of God, I venerate you for the holy virtues which, through the grace and light of the Holy Spirit, you bring into the hearts of your clients to change them from unfaithful Christians to faithful children of God.

—St. Francis of Assisi († 1126)

Mary, Queen and Intercessor

POWERFUL, sovereign Queen, come to our aid. Speak for us to our Lord Jesus Christ. Who can do it better than you who conversed with Him so intimately here on earth, and now so fully possess Him in heaven?

Speak to your Son for us. He cannot refuse you anything. Ask for us a great love of God, perseverance in His holy grace, and the happiness of dying in His friendship that we may see you and thank you with Him eternally.

—St. Bernard († 1153)

Mary, Glory of Mothers

YOU are blessed among women, O Co-redemptrix! Blessed One selected in preference to all who are blessed! Chosen One, singular among all who are chosen! Priceless Pearl that belongs in the treasury of God's wisdom! Mother, you are the Glory of Mothers!

We seek you, O Lady, and in all sincerity turn to you in prayer. Help us in our weakness; turn away from us all disgrace. Who is more worthy of entreating the Heart of our Lord Jesus Christ than you, blessed Mary, who live with your Son and speak with Him?

Speak, Mother, for your Son listens to you; and whatever you desire you will receive. Invoke His holy name in our behalf.

—St. Bernard († 1153)

Mary, Mother of God

WHEN God in His mercy was pleased to dwell among us, you alone, O Mary, were privileged to offer the King of kings and the Lord of lords a worthy dwelling in your virginal abode. Truly even God was delighted to remain with you. Rejoice, Virgin most blessed, Mother undefiled, all shall call you blessed.

Mary, the whole world reveres you as the holiest Shrine of the living God, for in you the salvation of the world saw its dawning. The Son of God was pleased to take human form from you. You have broken down the wall of hatred, the barrier between heaven and earth which was set up by man's first disobedience. In you heaven met earth when divinity and humanity were joined in one Person, the God-Man.

Mother of God, we sing your praises, but we must praise you even more. Our speech is too feeble to honor you as we ought, for no tongue is eloquent enough to express your excellence.

Mary, most powerful, most holy, worthy of all love! Your name brings new life, and the thought of you arouses love in the hearts of those who are devoted to you.

—St. Bernard († 1153)

Dedication to Mary

VIRGIN full of goodness, Mother of mercy, I entrust to you my body and soul, my thoughts, my actions, my life and my death.

O my Queen, help me, and deliver me from all the snares of the devil. Obtain for me the grace of loving my Lord Jesus Christ, your

Son, with a true and perfect love, and, after Him, O Mary, to love you with all my heart and above all things.

—St. Thomas Aquinas († 1274)

For a Happy Death

HOLY Virgin, I beg of you, when my soul shall depart from my body, be pleased to meet and receive it.

Mary, do not refuse me then the grace of being sustained by your sweet presence. Be for me the ladder and the way to heaven, and finally assure me of pardon and eternal rest.

—St. Bonaventure († 1274)

Little Psalms to Mary

MOTHER, you are our refuge in need, and our strength against our enemy.

Preserve your children from all evil; let them enjoy the shelter of your peace and love.

May we ever rely on the power of your name; and let all our deeds be directed to you.

Have pity on us, Mother, and show us your mercy, for you are the hope and the light of all who trust in you.

Your mercy and kindness are proclaimed everywhere; God has blessed the works of your hands.

* * *

MOTHER of our Savior, have pity on us; grant us consolation in our trials.

Present our cause to our Lord, and spare us all further distress.

Turn away from us the just displeasure of God; appease Him by your merits and prayers.

Heal the contrite of heart, Mother of our salvation, and refresh them with the balm of your motherly love.

Deliver us from our fears, Mother, and sweeten all our pain.

In you are salvation and life; unending joy and a glorious eternity.

Shed upon us the rays of your kindness, and enlighten us with the splendors of your compassion.

Be gracious to your children, and do not allow them to be overcome in their temptations.

* * *

MARY, full of grace, the Lord is with you; through you salvation was brought to the world.

Enrich us with the wealth of your graces, and with your loving consolations relieve our troubled souls.

Watch over us, Mother, and protect us from evil; be with us to the very end and we shall find eternal life.

We beg you let those who invoke your help in their needs find grace with God.

Show us your tender mercy, Mother, and we shall be refreshed on this earthly pilgrimage of life.

* * *

I SHALL call upon you, Mother of God, and you will hear me; your praises will gladden my heart.

I have called to you in trouble, and you have heard me at your throne in heaven.

Take up my cause, Mother, for I have departed from my innocence, but because I have hoped in you I shall not lose my soul.

To you, Mother, have I pleaded after having wandered from God, and I was saved by the power of your intercession.

In you, Mother, I place all my hope, because of your most loving compassion.

Into your hands I entrust my soul and body, my whole life and the hour of my death.

Intercede for us, Mother of God and Mediatrix, who have brought salvation to mankind.

* * *

BEHOLD our misery, glorious Virgin, and do not delay to aid us in temptation.

Remember to intercede for us with your Son, and turn away from us His just displeasure.

Be mindful, Mother of the poor and the unfortunate; support them by your refreshing help.

In dangers and doubts grant your aid; in all trials may we find your gracious presence.

Have pity on us, Mother, and show us your mercy, for you are the hope and the light of all who trust in you.

* * *

HAVE pity on us, Mother, and heal the wounds of our souls; remove the sorrow and worries of our souls.

Console us in our day of suffering; enlighten us by your wisdom.

Show us your mercy, Mother, and pray for us; turn our sadness into true joy.

Fill our hearts with your sweetness and make us forget the miseries of this life.

Be gracious to your children, and do not allow them to be overcome in their temptations.

* * *

YOU are glorious, Mother, and most worthy of praise, in the City of our God and in the Church of His elect.

You were assumed into heaven accompanied by angelic choirs, borne up by archangels and crowned with glory.

Have pity on us, Queen of glory and honor, and keep our souls from all danger.

As our prayer rises up to your throne, hear our humble pleas.

—St. Bonaventure († 1274)

Favor with God

DO NOT be afraid, Mary, for you have found favor with God" (Lk 1:30). Fear not, Mary, for you have found, not taken grace, as Lucifer tried to take it. You have not lost it, as Adam lost it. You have found favor with God because you have desired and sought it. You have found uncreated grace: that is, God Himself became your Son, and with that grace you have found and obtained every uncreated good.

—St. Albert the Great († 1280)

Petition to Mary

MOST chaste Virgin Mary, I beg of you, by that unspotted purity with which you prepared for the Son of God a dwelling of delight in your virginal womb, that by your intercession I may be cleansed from every stain.

Most humble Virgin Mary, I beg of you, by that most profound humility by which you deserved to be raised high above all the choirs of angels and saints, that by your intercession all my sins may be expiated.

Most amiable Virgin Mary, I beg of you, by that indescribable love which united you so closely and inseparably to God, that by your intercession I may obtain an abundance of all merits.

—St. Gertrude († 1334)

Offering to Mary

MOST holy Mary, Virgin Mother of God, most unworthy though I am to be your servant, yet moved by your motherly care for me and longing to serve you, I choose you this day to be my Queen, my Advocate and my Mother. I firmly resolve ever to be devoted to you and to do what I can to encourage others to be devoted to you.

My loving Mother, through the Precious Blood of your Son shed for me, I beg you to receive me as your servant forever. Aid me in my actions and beg for me the grace never by word or deed or thought to be displeasing in your sight and that of your most holy Son.

Remember me, dearest Mother, and do not abandon me at the hour of death.

—St. Francis de Sales († 1622)

The Spirit of Mary

HAIL MARY, beloved Daughter of the eternal Father. Hail Mary, wonderful Mother of the Son. Hail Mary, faithful Spouse of the Holy Spirit.

Hail Mary, my dear Mother, my loving Lady, my powerful Queen. You are all mine through your mercy, and I am all yours. Take away from me all that may be displeasing to God. Cultivate in me everything that is pleasing to you.

May the light of your faith dispel the darkness of my mind, your deep humility take the place of my pride; your continual sight of God fill my memory with His presence; the fire of the charity of your heart inflame the lukewarmness of my own heart; your virtues take the place of my sins; your merits be my enrichment and make up for all that is wanting in me before God.

My beloved Mother, grant that I may have no other spirit but your spirit, to know Jesus Christ and His divine will and to praise and glorify the Lord; that I may love God with burning love like yours.

—St. Louis de Montfort († 1716)

Mary, Hope for Salvation

MOST holy and immaculate Virgin, my Mother, You are the Mother of my Lord, the Queen of the world, the advocate, hope, and refuge of sinners. I, the most miserable among them, come to you today. I venerate you, great Queen, and thank you for the many graces you have bestowed on me. I thank you especially for having saved me so many times from the punishment of God which I deserved.

I love you, most lovable Lady. By the love which I have for you, I promise ever to serve you, and to do as much as I can to make you loved by others.

I put all my hope in you, my entire salvation. Receive me as your servant, Mother of mercy, and cover me with the mantle of your protection. Since you are so powerful with God, free me from all temptations, or, at least, obtain for me the grace to overcome them until death.

I ask of you a true love for Jesus Christ. Through you I hope to die a good death. My Mother, by the love you have for God, I beg you to help me always, and most of all at the last moment of my life. Do not leave me until you see me safe in heaven. I hope to thank and praise you there forever.

—St. Alphonsus Liguori († 1787)

Mary, Help of Christians

MARY, powerful Virgin, you are the mighty and glorious protector of the Church. You are the marvelous help of Christians. You are awe-inspiring as an army in battle array. You have destroyed heresy in the world.

In the midst of our anguish, our struggle and our distress, defend us from the power of the enemy, and at the hour of our death receive our soul in heaven.

—St. John Bosco († 1888)

Part 3

SPECIAL DEVOTIONS
TO MARY

"Holy Mary, Mother of God, pray for us now
and at the hour of our death."

SPECIAL DEVOTIONS
TO MARY

Immaculate Mother of God

IMMACULATE Virgin, Mother of God and my Mother, from your sublime throne in heaven turn upon me your eyes of pity. Filled with confidence in your goodness, and knowing full well your power, I beg you to extend to me your helping hand in this journey of life, which is so full of dangers for my soul.

In order that I may never be the slave of the devil through sin, but may ever live with a humble and pure heart, I entrust myself entirely to you. I consecrate my heart to you forever, my only desire being to love your divine Son Jesus.

Mary, none of your devout servants has ever perished. May I, too, be saved.

* * *

YOU are all fair, Mary, and the original stain is not in you. You are the glory of Jerusalem, you are the joy of Israel, you are the great honor of our people, you are the advocate of sinners.

Virgin most prudent, Mother most merciful, pray for us, intercede for us with our Lord Jesus Christ.

Our Lady of the Miraculous Medal

IMMACULATE Virgin Mary, Mother of our Lord Jesus Christ, and our mother. Filled with the most lively confidence in your all-powerful and never failing intercession, manifested so often through the Miraculous Medal, I, your loving and trustful child, implore you to obtain for me the favor I earnestly ask, if it is beneficial to my immortal soul and the souls for whom I pray. *(Mention your request)*.

You know, Mary, how often my soul has been the sanctuary of your Son Who hates evil. Obtain for me, then, a deep hatred of sin and that purity of heart which will unite me to God alone, so that my every thought, word, and deed may tend to His greater glory.

Obtain for me also the spirit of prayer and self-denial, that I may recover by penance what I have lost by sin, and at last reach that blessed home where you are the Queen of Angels and of men.

Virgin Mother of God, Mary Immaculate, I dedicate and consecrate myself to you under the title of Our Lady of the Miraculous Medal. May this medal be a sure sign of your affection for me and a constant reminder of my duties toward you. While wearing it, may I ever be blessed by your loving protection and preserved in the grace of your Son.

Most powerful Virgin, Mother of our Savior, keep me close to you every moment of my life. Obtain for me, your child, the grace of a happy death, so that, in union with you, I may enjoy the bliss of heaven forever.

Mary, conceived without sin, pray for us who have recourse to you.

Mediatrix of Grace

MOST holy Mary, Queen of heaven, treasure of life and everflowing channel of divine grace, by the sublime virtues, infused into your soul at your Immaculate Conception, you were so pleasing in the sight of God that you were privileged to conceive in your virginal womb the very Author of life and of grace, Jesus Christ, our Lord. By becoming the Mother of the God-Man, you also became the Mother of redeemed humanity.

Mother of grace and life, of mercy and forgiveness, turn to me your kind face. Behold my needs of body and soul. Keep me in the friendship of God and obtain for me the grace of final perseverance. With the help of your intercession, I am sure to obtain from your Divine Son all the graces necessary to serve God faithfully with all the powers of my soul and body. Thus you will show yourself to be the Mother of Divine Grace. Through the graces obtained by you, may I be able to live in holiness on earth, and enjoy the happiness of praising God with you in heaven.

Mother, I put all my trust in you. I rely entirely upon you because I love you sincerely.

Mary, Virgin Mother of God, pray to Jesus for me.

Immaculate Spouse of the Holy Spirit

BLESSED Virgin Mary, Mother of Jesus and my mother, I venerate you as the Immaculate Spouse of the Holy Spirit. You are the glory of Jerusalem, the joy of Israel, the honor of our people. As the valiant woman you crushed the head of the serpent when you offered your Divine Son to the heavenly Father in the love of the Holy Spirit for the salvation of the world. Through the merits of this precious sacrifice and through the sufferings of your Son, obtain for me the gifts of the Holy Spirit.

I thank the Holy Spirit for having chosen you as His Spouse and made you the dispenser of His graces. Look upon me with your compassionate eyes. See my distress and my needs. Help me that I may never lose the grace of God nor defile the temple of the Holy Spirit, that my soul may ever remain His holy dwelling. Pray for me that the Holy Spirit may come to me so that Christ may be formed in me. I beg you to dispose my heart for the graces of the Holy Spirit, Who has chosen you to be His Bride.

Purest and holiest heart of Mary, in whom Jesus lives through the Holy Spirit, implore for me from this Holy Spirit, that the Sacred Heart of Jesus, through Him, may live in my heart and in the hearts of all men.

* * *

MOST holy Virgin of the Cenacle, our Mother, Mary Immaculate, obtain for us, we humbly pray, the gifts of the Holy Spirit, that we may live in love and persevere in prayer, under your guidance and teaching, to the greater glory of God. May we work by word and deed for the salvation of souls, and deserve to enter into everlasting life.

Graciously be near us in our present needs, Our Lady of the Cenacle. Help us by your power, that Almighty God may be pleased to grant us, through your pleading, the favor for which we earnestly pray.

Our Lady of the Most Blessed Sacrament

VIRGIN Immaculate, Mother of Jesus and our Mother, we invoke you under the title of Our Lady of the Most Blessed Sacrament because you are the Mother of the Savior Who is present in the Eucharist. From you He received the flesh and blood with which He feeds us in Holy Communion.

We also invoke you under that title because the grace of the Eucharist comes to us through you, since you are the channel through which God's graces reach us, because you were the first to live the Eucharistic life.

Teach us to pray the Mass as you did, to receive Holy Communion frequently, and to adore our Lord in the Blessed Sacrament with some of your love and devotion.

You are the perfect lover of our Lord in the Eucharist. Grant us the grace to know Him better, to love Him more, and to center our lives around the Eucharist.

Virgin Mary, Our Lady of the Most Holy Sacrament, glory of the Christian people, joy of the universal Church, salvation of the world, pray for us and grant to all the faithful true devotion to the Most Holy Eucharist, that they may become worthy to receive it daily.

Immaculate Heart of Mary

MARY, Virgin most powerful and Mother of mercy, Queen of heaven and Refuge of sinners, we consecrate ourselves to your Immaculate Heart. We consecrate to you our very being and our whole life; all that we have, all that we love, all that we are. To you we give our bodies, our hearts, and our souls; to you we give our homes, our families, our country. We desire that all that is in us and around us may belong to you, and may share in the benefits of your motherly blessing.

That this act of consecration may be truly fruitful and lasting, we renew this day at your feet the promises of our baptism and our first Holy Communion.

We pledge ourselves to profess courageously and at all times the truths of our holy Faith, and to live as befits Catholics who are submissive to all the directions of the Pope and the Bishops in communion with him. We pledge ourselves to keep the commandments of God and His Church, in particular to keep holy the Lord's Day. We likewise pledge ourselves to make consoling practices of the Christian religion, and, above all, Holy Communion, an important part of our lives, in so far as we shall be able to do so.

Finally, we promise you, O glorious Mother of God and loving Mother of men, to devote ourselves wholeheartedly to the spreading of devotion to your Immaculate Heart, in order to hasten and assure, through the queenly rule of your Immaculate Heart, the coming of the kingdom of the Sacred Heart of your adorable

Son, in our own hearts and in those of all men, in our country and in all the world, as in heaven so on earth.

* * *

IMMACULATE Heart of Mary, full of love of God and men, I consecrate myself entirely to you. I entrust to you the salvation of my soul. With your help may I hate sin, love God and my neighbor, and reach eternal life together with those whom I love.

Mediatrix of Grace and Mother of Mercy, your Divine Son has merited boundless treasures of grace by His sufferings, which He has confided to you for us, your children. Filled with confidence in your motherly Heart, I come to you with my pressing needs. For the sake of the Sacred Heart of Jesus, obtain for me the favor I ask. *(Mention your request.)*

Dearest Mother, if what I ask for should not be according to God's will, pray that I may receive that which will be greater benefit to my soul. May I experience the kindness of your motherly Heart and the power of your intercession with Jesus during life and at the hour of my death.

Mother of Sorrows

MARY, most holy Virgin and Queen of Martyrs, accept the sincere homage of my childlike love. Into your heart, pierced by

so many sorrows, welcome my poor soul.
Receive it as the companion of your sorrows at
the foot of the cross, on which Jesus died for
the redemption of the world.

Sorrowful Virgin, with you I will gladly suffer all the trials, misunderstandings, and pains
which it shall please our Lord to send me. I
offer them all to you in memory of your sorrows, so that every thought of my mind, and
every beat of my heart, may be an act of compassion and of love for you.

Loving Mother, have pity on me, reconcile
me to your Divine Son Jesus, keep me in His
grace and assist me in my last agony, so that I
may be able to meet you in heaven and sing
your glories.

Mary most sorrowful, Mother of Christians,
pray for us. Mother of love, of sorrow and of
mercy, pray for us.

Mary Assumed into Heaven

MARY, my dear Mother and mighty
Queen, take and receive my poor heart
with all its freedom and desires, all its love and
all the virtues and graces with which it may be
adorned. All I am, all I might be, all I have and
hold in the order of nature as well as of grace,
I have received from God through your loving
intercession, my Lady and Queen. Into your

sovereign hands I entrust it all, that it may be returned to its noble origin.

Mary, Queen of every heart, accept all that I am and bind me to you with the bonds of love, that I may be yours forever, and may be able to say in all truth: "I belong to Jesus through Mary."

My Mother most pure, I love you. Give me love for you and for Jesus.

Queen of the universe, Mary ever Virgin, obtain peace and salvation for us through your prayers, for you have given birth to Christ the Lord, the Savior of all mankind.

Mother of Perpetual Help

MOTHER of Perpetual Help, you are the dispenser of every grace that God grants us. For this reason He made you so powerful and so kind, that you may help us in our needs. You are the advocate of sinners who come to you for help.

Come to aid me, for I entrust myself to your care. In your hands I place my eternal salvation. Take me under your protection and keep me as your faithful servant. If you protect me, I have nothing to fear; not my sins, for you will obtain pardon for them; not the evil spirits, for you are mightier than all the powers of hell; not even Jesus, my Judge, for He is appeased by your prayer. I fear only that through my own negligence I may forget to recommend myself to you.

Mother of Perpetual Help, obtain for me the forgiveness of my sins, love for Jesus, final perseverance, and the grace to turn to you for help at all times.

Mother of Mercy

MOST gracious Mother of Mercy, you are our light in uncertainty, our comfort in sorrow, our consolation in trial, our refuge from every danger and temptation. After your Divine Son, you are our sure hope of salvation.

I beg of you, listen graciously to my prayers. Give me true sorrow for my sins and obtain God's forgiveness for me through your prayers.

Mary, Mother of grace and Mother of Mercy, protect us from our enemy, and receive us at the hour of our death.

Mother of God and Mother of Mercy, pray for us and for all who have died in the embrace of the Lord.

My Mother, my Hope!

* * *

IMMACULATE Virgin, refuge of sinners, in order to atone for the injuries done to Almighty God and the evils inflicted on men by sin, you accepted with resignation the death of your Divine Son. Have pity on us, and in heaven where you reign gloriously, continue in our behalf your work of zeal and love.

We want to be your children. Show yourself a mother. Obtain from Jesus, our Divine Redeemer, that he may be pleased to apply to our souls the fruits of His Passion and death, and deliver us from the bonds of our sins. May He be our light in the midst of darkness, our strength in weakness, our refuge in peril. May He strengthen us by His grace and love in this world, and grant us the grace to love Him, see Him, and possess Him in the world to come.

Queen of the Holy Rosary

QUEEN of the most holy Rosary, in these times of such bold impiety, show your power, and from your throne, from which you bestow pardon and graces, mercifully look upon the Church of your Son, His Vicar on earth, the clergy and laity, who are sorely oppressed in this conflict.

You can overcome all heresies. Hasten the hour of mercy, even though the hour of God's justice is provoked by the sins of men.

Obtain for me the grace I need to live a holy life upon earth and to reign among the just in heaven. Together with all faithful Christians in the world, I greet you and acclaim you as Queen of the most holy Rosary.

Queen of the most holy Rosary, pray for us.

Queen of Peace

MOST holy Virgin, Mother of God and our Mother, by your divine maternity you merited to share in your Divine Son's prerogative of universal kingship.

We, your devoted children are comforted by the thought that as it pleased the Redeemer of mankind to have Himself announced by the prophets and by the angels at Bethlehem under the glorious title of King of Peace, so too it must be pleasing to you to hear yourself greeted and honored by us under the title of Queen of Peace, a title that is so dear to your motherly heart.

May your powerful intercession ward off from your people all hatred and discord. Direct our hearts in the ways of peace and brotherhood, which Jesus Christ came to teach among men for the salvation of all.

Crown with success the fatherly care with which the Holy Father, the Vicar on earth of your Divine Son, continually seeks to call together all the nations to God, the Giver of Peace.

Enlighten the rulers of all countries that they may maintain peace in the world.

"Mother of the Church, pray for us."

Part 4

GENERAL PRAYERS

CONSECRATION

Hail, Holy Queen

HAIL, holy Queen, Mother of mercy; hail our life, our sweetness, and our hope. To you do we cry, poor banished children of Eve. To you do we send up our sighs, mourning, and weeping in this valley of tears.

Turn then, most gracious Advocate, your eyes of mercy toward us. And after this our exile show unto us the blessed fruit of your womb, Jesus. O clement, O loving, O sweet Virgin Mary.

Memorare

REMEMBER, most gracious Virgin Mary, that never was it known that anyone who fled to your protection, implored your help or sought your intercession, was left unaided.

Inspired with this confidence, I fly to you, Virgin of virgins, my Mother. To you I come, before you I stand, sinful and sorrowful. Mother of the Word Incarnate, despise not my petitions, but in your mercy hear and answer me.

(St. Bernard)

The Angelus

THE angel of the Lord declared unto Mary, and she conceived of the Holy Spirit. Hail Mary.

Behold the handmaid of the Lord. Be it done to me according to your word. Hail Mary.

And the Word was made flesh, and dwelt among us. Hail Mary.

Pray for us, O Holy Mother of God, that we may be made worthy of the promises of Christ.

Let us pray. Pour forth, we beseech You, O Lord, Your grace into our hearts; that we, who have known the Incarnation of Christ Your Son by the message of an angel, may by His Passion and Cross be brought to the glory of His Resurrection; through the same Christ our Lord. Amen.

Marian Antiphons
(Advent-Christmas)

O LOVING Mother of our Savior, the open gate leading us to heaven, and Star of the Sea, hasten to aid us—we who fall but seek to rise again. You brought forth your Maker, Who is your Holy Lord, while all nature gazed in awe and wonder, Virgin ever, after, as before, through the mouth of Gabriel heaven spoke its Ave, have compassion on us sinners.

Even after giving birth, you remained a Virgin. Mother of God intercede for us.

Let us pray. God, Who through the virginity of the Blessed Mary gave all men the riches of eternal salvation, we entreat You to let us feel the intercession of her who gave us the Author of Life, our Lord Jesus Christ, Your Son.

(Lent)

HAIL, Queen of heaven; hail, mistress of the angels; hail, root of Jesse; hail, the gate through which the Light rose over the earth. Rejoice, virgin most renowned and of unsurpassed beauty.

Let me praise you, most holy Virgin, give me strength against your enemies.

Let us pray. God of mercy, be the support of our weakness and we shall celebrate in fitting manner the memory of the holy Mother of God; thus by her intercession may we rise from our sins! Through the same Christ our Lord.

(Easter)

QUEEN of heaven, rejoice, alleluia. The Son Whom you merited to bear, alleluia, has risen as He said, alleluia.

Rejoice and be glad, Virgin Mary, alleluia, for the Lord has truly risen, alleluia.

Let us pray. God, through the resurrection of Your Son, our Lord Jesus Christ, You deigned to fill the world with joy; grant, we beg of You, that through His Virgin Mother Mary, we may enjoy eternal life. Through the same Christ our Lord.

Consecration

MY QUEEN, my mother, I give myself entirely to you, and to show my devotion to you I consecrate to you my eyes, my ears, my mouth, my heart, and my whole being.

Therefore, loving Mother, as I am your own, keep me, guard me, as your property and possession.

* * *

MOST holy Mary, my Lady, to your blessed trust and special protection, and into the bosom of your mercy, I this day, every day, and in the hour of my death, commend my soul and my body.

To you I entrust all my worries and miseries, my life and the end of my life, that by your most holy intercession and by your merits all my actions may be directed and disposed according to your will and that of your Divine Son.

* * *

HOLIEST Virgin, with all my heart I praise you above all the angels and saints in heaven as the Daughter of the Eternal Father, and to you I consecrate my soul and all its powers.

Hail Mary . . .

Holiest Virgin, with all my heart I praise you above all the angels and saints as the Mother of the only-begotten Son, and to you I consecrate my body with all its senses.

Hail Mary . . .

Holiest Virgin, with all my heart I praise you above all the angels and saints in heaven as the Spouse of the Holy Spirit, and to you I consecrate my heart and all its affections, praying you to obtain for me from the Ever-Blessed Trinity all the graces which I need for my salvation.

Hail Mary . . .

Consecration of the Family

DEAR Jesus, Mary, and Joseph, to you we consecrate our family and all that we have. We want our home to belong entirely to you. You made family life holy by your family life at Nazareth. Your home was a home of prayer, love, patient endurance, and toil.

It is our earnest wish to model our home upon yours at Nazareth. Remain with us, so that with your help the purity of our morals may be preserved, that we may obey the commandments of God and of the Church, and receive the sacraments frequently.

Willingly we surrender our entire freedom to you, our Queen and our Mother. We place under your care, our body and its senses, our soul and its faculties, our thoughts and desires, our words and deeds, our joys and sorrows, our life and our death.

Give your aid to our family, to our relatives, and to all who do us good. Under your guidance may we always follow the Holy Spirit and never hinder His grace in us through sin.

Help us to tread our way successfully through the dangers of this life and so win passage to our home country in heaven. As saints there with you, may we sing the praises of each Person of the Blessed Trinity for all eternity.

Keep love and peace in our midst. Console us in our troubles. Help us to preserve the innocence of our children. Enlighten and strengthen our growing sons and daughters. Assist us all at the hour of death, so that we may be united with each other and with you in heaven.

Petition

HOLY and glorious Virgin Mary, beautiful daughter of the Father, influential Mother of the Word, heavenly Bride of the

Holy Spirit, gentle Queen of the faithful, safe Refuge of sinners, perfect Model of all who are in the state of grace! God the Father and the Son love you with eternal affection in the Holy Spirit. The Heart of Jesus fills you with His own spirit and love. One with St. Joseph and all the angels and saints of God, we cherish you with a special love.

Your children delight your heart. We join them as they offer their work and prayers to you in all parts of the world. May we too please you with our zeal in prayer and patient perseverance in work.

We thank the Holy Spirit for choosing you as His immaculate Bride, for making you the Mother of God and the Channel of all grace.

May the entire Church feel your aid. Help our Holy Father, all bishops, priests, religious, and all the Catholic laity. Keep watch over sinners, over those wandering in error and unbelief, over the souls in purgatory.

Litany

LORD, have mercy. *Christ, have mercy.*
Lord, have mercy.
Christ, hear us. *Christ, graciously hear us.*
God the Father of Heaven, *have mercy on us.*
God the Son, Redeemer of the world,
God the Holy Spirit,
Holy Trinity, one God,
Holy Mary, *pray for us.*

Holy Mother of God,
Holy Virgin of virgins,
Mother of Christ,
Mother of Divine grace,
Mother most pure,
Mother most chaste,
Mother inviolate,
Mother undefiled,
Mother most amiable,
Mother most admirable,
Mother of good counsel,
Mother of our Creator,
Mother of our Savior,
Virgin most prudent,
Virgin most venerable,
Virgin most renowned,
Virgin most powerful,
Virgin most merciful,
Virgin most faithful,
Mirror of justice,
Seat of wisdom,
Cause of our joy,
Spiritual vessel,
Vessel of honor,
Singular vessel of devotion,
Mystical rose,
Tower of David,
Tower of ivory,
House of gold,
Ark of the covenant,
Gate of heaven,
Morning star,

Health of the sick,
Refuge of sinners,
Comfort of the afflicted,
Help of Christians,
Queen of Angels,
Queen of Patriarchs,
Queen of Prophets,
Queen of Apostles,
Queen of Martyrs,
Queen of Confessors,
Queen of Virgins,
Queen of all Saints,
Queen conceived without original sin,
Queen assumed into heaven,
Queen of the most holy Rosary,
Queen of Peace,
Lamb of God, who take away the sins of the world, *spare us, O Lord.*
Lamb of God, who take away the sins of the world, *graciously hear us, O Lord.*
Lamb of God, who take away the sins of the world, *have mercy on us.*
℣. Pray for us, holy Mother of God.
℟. That we may be made worthy of the promises of Christ.

Let us pray. Grant, we beg You, O Lord God, that we Your servants may rejoice in continual health of mind and body. Through the glorious intercession of Blessed Mary ever Virgin, may we be freed from present sorrow and enjoy eternal gladness. Through Christ our Lord. Amen.

Part 5

THE SCRIPTURAL ROSARY

The Rosary of the Blessed Virgin Mary, according to the tradition accepted by our predecessor Saint Pius V and authoritatively taught by him, consists of various elements disposed in an organic fashion:

a) Contemplation, in communion with Mary, of a series of *mysteries of salvation*, wisely distributed into three cycles. These mysteries express the joy of the Messianic times, the salvific suffering of Christ and the glory of the Risen Lord which fills the Church. This contemplation by its very nature encourages practical reflection and provides norms for living.

b) The *Lord's Prayer*, or Our Father, which by reason of its immense value is at the basis of Christian prayer and ennobles that prayer in its various expressions.

c) The litany-like succession of the *Hail Mary*, which is made up of the Angel's greeting to the Virgin (cf. Lk 1:28) and of Elizabeth's greeting (cf. Lk 1:42), followed by the ecclesial supplication Holy Mary. The continued series of Hail Marys is the special characteristic of the Rosary, and their number, in the full and typical number of one hundred and fifty, presents a certain analogy with the Psalter and is an element that goes back to the very origin of the exercise of piety. But this number, divided, according to a well-tried custom, into decades attached to the individual mysteries, is distributed in the three cycles already mentioned, thus giving rise to the Rosary of fifty Hail Marys as we know it. This latter has entered into use as the normal measure of the pious exercise and as such has been adopted by popular piety and approved by papal authority, which also enriched it with numerous indulgences.

d) The doxology *Glory be to the Father* which, in conformity with an orientation common to Christian piety, concludes the prayer with the glorifying of God Who is One and Three, from Whom, through Whom and in Whom all things have their being (cf. Rom 11:36).

These are the elements of the Rosary. Each has its own particular character which, wisely understood and appreciated, should be reflected in the recitation, in order that the Rosary may express all its richness and variety. Thus the recitation will be grave and supplicant during the Lord's Prayer, lyrical and full of praise during the tranquil succession of Hail Marys, contemplative in the recollected meditation on the mysteries and full of adoration during the doxology. This applies to all the ways in which the Rosary is usually recited: privately, in intimate recollection with the Lord; in community, in the family or in groups of the faithful gathered together to ensure the special presence of the Lord (cf. Mt 18:20); or publicly, in assemblies to which the ecclesial community is invited.

We now desire, as a continuation of the thought of our predecessors, to recommend strongly the recitation of the family Rosary. . . . There must logically follow a concrete effort to reinstate communal prayer in family life if there is to be a restoration of the theological concept of the family as the domestic Church.

In concluding these observations, which give proof of the concern and esteem which the Apostolic See has for the Rosary of the Blessed Virgin, we desire at the same time to recommend that this very worthy devotion should not be propagated in a way that is too one-sided or exclusive. The Rosary is an excellent prayer, but the faithful should feel serenely free in its regard. They should be drawn to its calm recitation by its intrinsic appeal.

Pope Paul VI on the Rosary

THE HOLY ROSARY

In the name of the Father, and of the Son, and of the Holy Spirit. Amen.

The Apostles' Creed

I believe in God, the Father almighty, Creator of heaven and earth, and in Jesus Christ, His only Son, our Lord, Who was conceived by the Holy Spirit, born of the Virgin Mary, suffered under Pontius Pilate, was crucified, died and was buried; He descended into hell; on the third day He rose again from the dead; He ascended into heaven, and is seated at the right hand of God the Father almighty; from there He will come to judge the living and the dead.

I believe in the Holy Spirit, the holy catholic Church, the communion of saints, the forgiveness of sins, the resurrection of the body, and life everlasting. Amen.

Faith, Hope, Charity

Our Father, . . .
For an increase of faith, hope and charity:
Hail Mary . . . *(3 times)*
Glory be . . .
Our Father, . . . *(before each mystery)*

*"O my Jesus, forgive us our sins, save us from the fire of hell, take all souls to heaven, and help especially those most in need of Your mercy." *(after each mystery)*

*In her second apparition at Fatima, June 13, 1917, our Lady taught three shepherd children to add this invocation after each decade of the Rosary.

THE JOYFUL MYSTERIES OF THE ROSARY

1. *The Annunciation*

1. The angel Gabriel was sent by God to a town of Galilee called Nazareth, to a virgin betrothed to a man named Joseph, of the house of David. The virgin's name was Mary.

2. The angel came to her and said, "Hail, full of grace! The Lord is with you."

3. She was greatly troubled by his words and wondered in her heart what this salutation could mean.

4. Then the angel said to her, "Do not be afraid, Mary, for you have found favor with God."

5. "Behold, you will conceive in your womb and bear a Son, and you will name Him Jesus."

6. "He will be great and will be called Son of the Most High. The Lord God will give Him the throne of His ancestor David. He will rule over the house of Jacob forever, and of his kingdom there will be no end."

7. Mary said to the angel, "How will this be, since I am a virgin?"

8. The angel answered, "The Holy Spirit will come upon you, and the power of the Most High will overshadow you. Therefore the child

to be born will be holy, and He will be called the Son of God."

9.   "And behold, your cousin Elizabeth in her old age has also conceived a son, she who was called barren is now in her sixth month, for nothing will be impossible for God."

10.   Mary said, "Behold, I am the servant of the Lord. Let it be done to me according to your word." After this, the angel departed from her. (Lk 1:26-38)

Glory be . . . *(after each mystery)*

2. *The Visitation*

1.   Mary set out and journeyed in haste into the hill country to a town of Judah where she entered the house of Zechariah and greeted Elizabeth.

2.   When Elizabeth heard Mary's greeting, the baby leaped in her womb.

3.   Elizabeth was filled with the Holy Spirit, and she exclaimed with a loud cry, "Blessed are you among women, and blessed is the fruit of your womb."

4.   "Why am I so greatly favored that the mother of my Lord should visit me? For behold, the moment that the sound of your greeting reached my ears, the child in my womb leaped for joy."

5. "Blessed is she who believed that what the Lord has said to her will be fulfilled."

6. And Mary said: "My soul proclaims the greatness of the Lord, my spirit rejoices in God my Savior."

7. "For He has looked with favor on the lowliness of His servant; henceforth all generations will call me blessed."

8. "The Mighty One has done great things for me; and holy is His name. His mercy is shown from age to age to those who fear Him."

9. "He has come to the aid of Israel His servant, ever mindful of His merciful love, according to the promises He made to our ancestors, to Abraham and his descendants forever."

10. Mary remained with Elizabeth about three months and then returned home. (Lk 1:39-56)

3. *The Birth of our Lord*

1. The birth of Jesus Christ occurred this way. When His Mother Mary was engaged to Joseph, but before they came to live together, she was found to be with child through the Holy Spirit.

2. Her husband Joseph was a just man and did not wish to expose her to the ordeal of public disgrace; therefore, he resolved to divorce her quietly.

3. After he had decided to follow this course of action, an angel of the Lord appeared to him in a dream and said, "Joseph, son of David, do not be afraid to receive Mary into your home as your wife."

4. "For this Child has been conceived in her womb through the Holy Spirit. She will give birth to a Son, and you shall name Him Jesus, because He will save His people from their sins."

5. All this took place in order to fulfill what the Lord had announced through the prophet: "Behold, the virgin shall conceive and give birth to a Son, and they shall name Him Emmanuel," a name which means "God is with us."

6. When Joseph rose from his sleep, he did what the angel of the Lord had commanded him. He took Mary into his home as his wife. (Mt 1:18-25)

7. Joseph therefore went from the town of Nazareth in Galilee to Judea, to the city of David called Bethlehem, because he was of the house and family of David. He went to be registered together with Mary, his betrothed, who was expecting a child.

8. While they were there, the time came for her to have her child, and she gave birth to her firstborn Son. She wrapped Him in swaddling clothes and laid Him in a manger, because there was no room for them in the inn. (Lk 2:4-7)

9.   The angel said to [the shepherds], "Do not be afraid, for I bring you good news of great joy for all the people. For this day in the city of David there has been born to you a Savior Who is Christ the Lord.

10.   Suddenly, there was with the angel a multitude of the heavenly host, praising God and saying, "Glory to God in the highest, and on earth peace to all those on whom His favor rests." (Lk 2:10-14)

4. *The Presentation in the Temple*

1.   When the days for their purification were completed according to the Law of Moses, they brought the Child up to Jerusalem to present Him to the Lord.

2.   At that time, there was a man in Jerusalem whose name was Simeon. The upright and devout man was awaiting the consolation of Israel, and the Holy Spirit rested on him.

3.   It had been revealed to him by the Holy Spirit that he would not experience death before he had seen the Christ of the Lord.

4.   Prompted by the Spirit, Simeon came into the temple. When the parents brought in the Child Jesus to do for Him what was required by the Law, he took Him in his arms and praised God.

5.   "Now, Lord, You may dismiss Your servant in peace, according to Your word."

6. "For my eyes have seen Your salvation, which you have prepared in the sight of all the peoples, a light of revelation to the Gentiles and the glory of Your people Israel."

7. The Child's father and mother marveled at what was being said about Him.

8. Simeon blessed them and said to Mary His Mother: "This Child is destined for the fall and rise of many in Israel, and to be a sign that will be opposed, so that the secret thoughts of many will be revealed, and you yourself a sword will pierce." (Lk 2:22-35)

9. When [the pair] had fulfilled everything required by the Law of the Lord, they returned to Galilee, to their own town of Nazareth.

10. The Child grew and became strong, filled with wisdom, and God's favor was upon Him. (Lk 2:39-40)

5. *The Finding of the Child Jesus in the Temple*

1. Every year His parents used to go to Jerusalem for the feast of Passover. And when Jesus was twelve years old, they made the journey as usual for the feast.

2. When the days of the feast were over and they set off for home, the boy Jesus stayed behind in Jerusalem. His parents were not aware of this.

3. Assuming that He was somewhere in the group of travelers, they journeyed for a day.

Then they started to look for Him among their relatives and friends.

4. When they failed to find Him, they returned to Jerusalem in search of Him.

5. After three days they found Him in the temple, where He was sitting among the teachers, listening to them and asking them questions. And all who heard Him were amazed at His intelligence and His answers.

6. When they saw Him, they were astonished, and His Mother said to Him: "Son, why have You done this to us? Your father and I have been searching for You with great anxiety."

7. Jesus said to them, "Why were you searching for me? Did you not know that I must be in My Father's house?"

8. But they did not comprehend what He said to them.

9. Then He went down with them and came to Nazareth, and He was obedient to them.

10. His Mother pondered all these things in her heart. And Jesus increased in wisdom and in age and in grace with God and men. (Lk 2:41-52)

THE LUMINOUS MYSTERIES
OF THE ROSARY

On October 16, 2002, Pope John Paul II issued an Apostolic Letter entitled *The Rosary of the Virgin Mary*, encouraging all Catholics to recite the Rosary. He also suggested five new Mysteries that might supplement the meditation on the traditional Joyful, Sorrowful, and Glorious Mysteries of the Rosary.

The new Mysteries, i.e., Mysteries of Light or the Luminous Mysteries, are intended to offer contemplation of important parts of Christ's Public Life in addition to the contemplation on His Childhood, His Sufferings, and His Risen Life offered by the traditional Mysteries: "Of the many Mysteries of Christ's life, only a few are indicated by the Rosary in the form that has become generally established with the seal of the Church's approval. . . .

"I believe, however, that to bring out fully the Christological depth of the Rosary it would be suitable to make an addition to the traditional pattern which, while left to the freedom of individuals and communities, could broaden it to include the Mysteries of Christ's Public Ministry between His Baptism and His Passion. In the course of those Mysteries we contemplate important aspects of the person of Christ as the definitive revelation of God. Declared the beloved Son of the Father at the Baptism in the Jordan, Christ is the One Who announces the coming of the Kingdom, bears witness to it in His works and proclaims its demands. It is during the years of His Public Ministry that the Mystery of Christ is most evidently a Mystery of Light: 'While I am in the world, I am the light of the world' (Jn 9:5).

"Consequently . . . it is fitting to add, following reflection on the Incarnation and the Hidden Life of Christ (the Joyful Mysteries) and before focusing on the sufferings of His Passion (the Sorrowful Mysteries) and the triumph of His Resurrection (the Glorious Mysteries), a meditation on certain particularly significant moments in His Public Ministry (the Mysteries of Light)."

The Pope assigned these new Mysteries to Thursday while transferring the Joyful Mysteries—normally said on that day—to Saturday because of the special Marian presence in them.

1. *The Baptism of Jesus*

1. Jesus arrived from Galilee and came to John at the Jordan to be baptized by him.
2. John tried to dissuade Him, saying, "Why do You come to me? I am the one who needs to be baptized by You."
3. But Jesus said to him in reply, "For the present, let it be thus. It is proper for us to do this to fulfill all that righteousness demands."
4. Then John acquiesced.
5. After Jesus had been baptized, as He came up from the water, the heavens were opened.

6.   And He beheld the Spirit of God descending like a dove and alighting on Him.

7.   And a voice came from heaven, saying, "This is My beloved Son, in Whom I am well pleased."

8.   [These words recall the words of the Lord spoken by the Prophet Isaiah about the Suffering Servant:] "This is My Servant Whom I uphold, My chosen one in Whom I delight." (Mt 3:13-17)

9.   "I will put My Spirit in Him, and He will bring justice to the nations.

10. "In His law the coastlands will place their hope. This is what the Lord says." (Isa 42:1-2, 4-5)

2. Christ's Self-Manifestation at Cana

1.   On the third day, there was a wedding feast at Cana in Galilee. The Mother of Jesus was there, and Jesus and His disciples had also been invited.

2.   When the wine was exhausted, the Mother of Jesus said to Him, "They have no wine."

3.   Jesus responded, "Woman, what concern is this to us? My hour has not yet come."

4.   His Mother said to the servants, "Do whatever He tells you."

5.   Standing nearby there were six stone water jugs of the type used for Jewish rites of purification, each holding twenty to thirty gallons.

6. Jesus instructed the servants, "Fill the jars with water."

7. When they had filled them to the brim, He ordered them, "Now draw some out and take it to the chief steward," and they did so.

8. When the chief steward had tasted the water that had become wine, he did not know where it came from, although the servants who had drawn the water knew.

9. The chief steward called over the bridegroom and said, "Everyone serves the choice wine first, and then an inferior vintage when the guests have had too much to drink. However, you have saved the best wine until now."

10. Jesus performed this, the first of His signs, at Cana in Galilee, thereby revealing His glory, and His disciples believed in Him. (Jn 2:1-11)

3. *Christ's Proclamation of the Kingdom of God*

1. Jesus said, "The time of fulfillment has arrived, and the Kingdom of God is close at hand. Repent, and believe in the Gospel."

2. Later, He gave them the eight Beatitudes: "Blessed are the poor in spirit, for theirs is the Kingdom of heaven.

3. "Blessed are those who mourn, for they will be comforted.

4. "Blessed are the meek, for they will inherit the earth.

5. "Blessed are those who hunger and thirst for justice, for they will have their fill.

6. "Blessed are the merciful, for they will obtain mercy.

7. "Blessed are the pure of heart, for they will see God.

8. "Blessed are the peacemakers, for they will be called children of God.

9. "Blessed are those who are persecuted in the cause of justice, for theirs is the Kingdom of heaven.

10. "Blessed are you when people insult you and persecute you and utter all kinds of calumnies against you for My sake. Rejoice and be glad, for your reward will be great in heaven." (Mk 1:14-15; Mt 5:3-12)

4. *The Transfiguration*

1. Six days later, Jesus took Peter and James and his brother John . . . with Him and led them up a high mountain by themselves.

2. And in their presence He was transfigured; His face shone like the sun, and His clothes became dazzling white.

3. Suddenly, there appeared to them Moses and Elijah, conversing with Him.

4. Then Peter said to Jesus, "Lord, it is good for us to be here.

5.   "If You wish, I will make three tents here—one for You, one for Moses, and one for Elijah."

6.   While he was speaking, suddenly a bright cloud cast a shadow over them.

7.   Then a voice from the cloud said, "This is My Beloved Son, with Whom I am well pleased. Listen to Him."

8.   When the disciples heard this, they fell on their faces and were greatly frightened.

9.   But Jesus came and touched them, saying, "Stand up, and do not be frightened."

10. And when they raised their eyes, they saw no one, but only Jesus. (Mt 17:1-8)

5. *Institution of the Eucharist*

1.   The day of the Feast of Unleavened Bread arrived, on which the Passover lamb had to be sacrificed.

2.   Jesus sent Peter and John, saying, "Go and make preparations for us to eat the Passover."

3.   When the hour came, Jesus took His place at table along with the Apostles.

4.   He said to them, "I have eagerly desired to eat this Passover with you before I suffer.

5.   "For I tell you, that from this moment on, I shall never eat it again, until it is fulfilled in the Kingdom of God."

6. Then He took the cup, and after giving thanks, He said, "Take this and divide it among yourselves.

7. "For I tell you, that from this moment, I will not drink of the fruit of the vine until the Kingdom of God comes."

8. Then He took bread, and after giving thanks He broke it and gave it to them, saying, "This is My Body, which will be given for you.

9. "Do this in memory of Me."

10. And He did the same with the cup after supper, saying, "This cup is the new covenant in My Blood, which will be poured out for you." (Lk 22:7-8, 14-20)

THE SORROWFUL MYSTERIES OF THE ROSARY

1. *The Agony in the Garden*

1. [Jesus and His disciples] went to a place that was called Gethsemane, and Jesus said to His disciples, "Sit here while I pray." He took with Him Peter and James and John.

2. He began to suffer distress and anguish. And He said to them, "My soul is sorrowful, even to the point of death. Remain here and keep watch."

3. Moving on a little farther, He threw Himself on the ground and prayed that, if it were possible, the hour might pass Him by.

4. [He kept] saying, "*Abba*, Father, for You all things are possible. Take this cup from Me. Yet not My will but Yours be done."

5. Returning to the disciples, He found them sleeping. He said to Peter, "Simon, are you asleep? Could you not keep watch for one hour? Stay awake and pray that you may not enter into temptation. The spirit is indeed willing but the flesh is weak."

6. Again He went apart and prayed, saying the same words. Then He came again and found them sleeping, for their eyes were heavy, and they did not know what to say to Him.

7. When He returned a third time, He said to them, "Are you still sleeping and taking your rest? Enough! The hour has come when the Son of Man is to be betrayed into the hands of sinners. Get up! Let us go! Look, My betrayer is approaching."

8. At once, while He was still speaking, Judas one of the Twelve, arrived. With him there was a crowd of men, armed with swords and clubs, who had been sent by the chief priests, the scribes, and the elders. (Mk 14:32-43)

9. [Jesus said,] "Why are you coming forth with swords and clubs as though I were a bandit? When I was with you day after day in the temple, you did not raise a hand against Me. But this is the hour for you and the power of darkness!"

10. Then they arrested Jesus and led Him away. They brought Him to the house of the high priest, and Peter followed at a distance. (Lk 22:52-54)

2. *The Scourging*

1. When the dawn came, the council of the elders of the people, both the chief priests and the scribes, assembled, and they brought Him before their Sanhedrin. Then they said, "If you are the Christ, tell us!"

2. He replied, "If I tell you, you will not believe; and if I question you, you will not answer. But from now on, the Son of Man will be seated at the right hand of the power of God." (Lk 22:66-69)

3. As soon as it was morning, the chief priests held a council with the elders and scribes and the whole Sanhedrin. They bound Jesus and led Him away, and handed Him over to Pilate. Pilate asked Him, "Are You the King of the Jews?" Jesus replied. "You have said so."

4. Then the chief priests brought many charges against Him. Again, Pilate questioned Him, "Have You no answer to offer? Just consider how many charges they are leveling against You." But Jesus offered no further reply, so that Pilate was amazed. (Mk 15:1-5)

5. However, the chief priests incited the crowd to have him release Barabbas for them

instead. Pilate then asked, "And what shall I do with the man you call the King of the Jews?" They shouted back, "Crucify Him!" (Mk 15:11-13)

6. [Barabbas] had been imprisoned for an insurrection that had occurred in the city as well as for murder. In his desire to release Jesus, Pilate again pleaded with them, but they continued to shout, "Crucify Him! Crucify Him!"

7. A third time he addressed them, "Why? What evil has He done? I have not found in Him any crime that deserves death. Therefore, I will have Him scourged and let Him go."

8. However, with loud shouts they continued to insist that He should be crucified, and their voices prevailed. (Lk 23:19-23)

9. And so Pilate, anxious to appease the crowd, released Barabbas to them.

10. And after ordering Jesus to be scourged, he handed Him over to be crucified. (Mk 15:15)

3. *The Crowning with Thorns*

1. Then the soldiers led Jesus away inside the palace, that is, the Praetorium, and they called the whole cohort together.

2. They dressed Him in a purple robe and after twisting some thorns into a crown, they placed it on Him.

3.   Then they began to salute Him with the words, "Hail, King of the Jews!"

4.   They repeatedly struck His head with a reed, and spat upon Him, and knelt down before Him in homage. (Mk 15:16-19)

5.   Once again, Pilate went out and said to the Jews, "Look, I am bringing Him out to you to let you know that I find no evidence of a crime in Him."

6.   Then Jesus came out, wearing the crown of thorns and the purple robe. Pilate said to them, "Behold, the Man!"

7.   When they saw Him, the chief priests and the temple guards shouted, "Crucify Him! Crucify Him!" (Jn 19:4-6)

8.   From that moment on, Pilate sought to release Him, but the Jews kept shouting, "If you release this Man, you are no Friend of Caesar. Everyone who claims to be a king opposes Caesar."

9.   When Pilate heard these words, he brought Jesus out and seated Him on the judge's bench at the place known as the Stone Pavement. . . . Pilate said to the Jews, "Behold, your King!"

10.   They shouted, "Away with Him! Away with Him! Crucify Him!" . . . Then he handed Him over to them to be crucified. (Jn 19:12-16)

4. *The Carrying of the Cross*

1. And when the soldiers had finished mocking Him, they stripped Him of the robe, dressed Him in His own clothes, and led Him away to crucify Him.

2. As they went out, they encountered a man of Cyrene named Simon, and they forced him to carry the cross. (Mt 27:31-32)

3. A large number of people followed Jesus, among them many women who were mourning and lamenting over Him.

4. He turned to them and said, "Daughters of Jerusalem, do not weep for Me. Weep rather for yourselves and for your children." (Lk 23:27-28)

5. There were also two others, both criminals, who were led away to be executed with Him. (Lk 23:32)

6. When they came to a place called Golgotha, which means place of the Skull, they offered Him some wine to drink that had been mixed with gall; but after tasting it, He refused to drink the mixture.

7. And after they had crucified Him, they divided His garments among them by casting lots. Then they sat down there to keep guard over Him.

8. Above His head was inscribed the charge against Him: "This is Jesus, King of the Jews."

9. Two thieves were crucified with Him, one on His right and the other on His left.

10. Those people who passed by jeered at Him, shaking their heads and saying, "You Who claimed You could destroy the temple and rebuild it within three days, save Yourself! If You truly are the Son of God, come down from the cross!" In much the same way, the chief priests, together with the scribes and the elders, joined in the mockery. (Mt 27:33-41)

5. *The Crucifixion*

1. Jesus said, "Father, forgive them, for they do not know what they are doing." (Lk 23:34)

2. [One of the criminals said,] "Jesus, remember me when You come into Your kingdom." Jesus said to him, "Amen, I say to you, today you will be with Me in paradise." (Lk 23:42-43)

3. When Jesus saw His Mother and the disciple whom He loved standing beside her, He said to His Mother, "Woman, behold, your son." Then He said to the disciple, "Behold, your Mother." And from that hour the disciple took her into his home. (Jn 19:26-27)

4. About three o'clock Jesus cried out in a loud voice, . . . "My God, My God, why have You forsaken Me?" (Mt 27:46)

5. After this, aware that everything had now

been completed, and in order that the Scripture might be fulfilled Jesus said, "I thirst." A jar filled with sour wine was standing nearby, so they soaked a sponge in the wine on a branch of hyssop and and held it up to His lips.

6.   When Jesus had taken the wine, He said, "It is finished." (Jn 19:28-30)

7.   Darkness came over the whole land until three in the afternoon, for the sun was darkened. Then the veil of the temple was torn in two. He cried out, "Father into Your hands I commend My spirit." And with these words He breathed His last. (Lk 23:44-46)

8.   When [the soldiers] came to Jesus and saw that He was already dead, they did not break His legs, but one of the soldiers thrust a lance into His side, and immediately a flow of blood and water came forth. (Jn 19:33-34)

9.   They took the body of Jesus and wrapped it with spices in linen cloths, in accordance with the burial custom of the Jews.

10.   At the place where Jesus had been crucified there was a garden, and in that garden there was a new tomb in which no one had ever been buried. And so, since it was the Jewish day of Preparation and the tomb was nearby, they laid Jesus there. (Jn 19:40-42)

THE GLORIOUS MYSTERIES
OF THE ROSARY

1. *The Resurrection*

1. After the Sabbath, at dawn on the first day of the week, Mary Magdalene and the other Mary went to visit the sepulcher.

2. And behold, there was a violent earthquake, for an angel of the Lord, descended from heaven, came and rolled back the stone and sat upon it. His face shone like lightning, and his garments were as white as snow.

3. The guards were so paralyzed with fear of him that they became like dead men.

4. But the angel said to the women, "Do not be afraid! I know that you are looking for Jesus Who was crucified. He is not here, for He has been raised, as He promised He would be."

5. "Come and see the place where He lay. Then go quickly and tell His disciples: 'He has been raised from the dead and now He is going ahead of you to Galilee. There you will see Him.' Behold, I have told you." (Mt 28:1-7)

6. Then [Jesus] said to [His disciples], "How foolish you are, and how slow to believe all that the Prophets have spoken! Was in not necessary that the Christ should suffer these things and enter into His glory?" (Lk 24:25-26)

7. Jesus Himself stood in their midst and said to them, "Peace be with you." Startled and ter-

rified, they thought that they were seeing a ghost. He said to them, "Why are you troubled, and why are doubts arising in your hearts? Look at My hands and My feet. It is I Myself. Touch Me and see. For a ghost does not have flesh and bones as you can see that I have." And when He had said this, He showed them His hands and His feet. (Lk 24:36-40)

8. Jesus said to Mary, "Do not hold on to Me, because I have not yet ascended to My Father. But go to My brethren and tell them, 'I am ascending to My Father and your Father, to My God and your God!' " (Jn 20:17)

9. The disciples were filled with joy when they saw the Lord. "Peace be with you," Jesus said to them again. "As the Father has sent Me, so I send you." After saying this, He breathed on them and said, "Receive the Holy Spirit. If you forgive anyone's sins, they are forgiven. If you retain anyone's sins, they are retained." (Jn 20:20-23)

10. Then [Jesus] said to Thomas, "Put your finger here and see My hands. Reach out your hand and put it into My side. Do not doubt any longer, but believe." Thomas exclaimed, "My Lord and my God!" Then Jesus said to him, "You have come to believe because you have seen Me. Blessed are those who have not seen and and yet have come to believe." (Jn 20:27-29)

2. *The Ascension*

1. Then [Jesus] led them out as far as Bethany, and lifting up His hands He blessed them. (Lk 24:50)

2. Jesus approached them and said, "All authority in heaven and on earth has been given to Me."

3. "Go, therefore, and make disciples of all nations, baptizing them in the name of the Father and of the Son and of the Holy Spirit, teaching them to observe all that I have commanded you."

4. "And behold, I am with you always, to the end of the world." (Mt 28:18-20)

5. "Whoever believes and is baptized will be saved; whoever does not believe will be condemned." (Mk 16:16)

6. While He was blessing them, He departed from them and was taken up to heaven. (Lk 24:51)

7. He was lifted up as they looked on, and a cloud took Him from their sight. While He was departing as they gazed upward toward the sky, suddenly two men dressed in white robes stood beside them.

8. "Men of Galilee, why are you standing there looking up into the sky? This Jesus Who has been taken up from you into heaven will come back in the same way you have seen Him going into heaven." (Acts 1:9-11)

9. They worshiped Him and then returned to Jerusalem filled with great joy, and they were continually in the temple praising God. (Lk 24:52-53)

10. [Jesus] took His place at the right hand of God. (Mk 16:20)

3. *The Descent of the Holy Spirit*

1. Jesus said, "I will ask the Father, and He will give you another Advocate to be with you always: the Spirit of truth, Whom the world cannot accept, since it neither sees Him nor recognizes Him."

2. "But you can recognize Him because He remains with you and will be with you forever. . . . I will not leave you orphans; I will come to you." (Jn 14:16-19)

3. "The Advocate, the Holy Spirit, Whom the Father will send in My name, will teach you everything and remind you of all that I have said to you." (Jn 14:26)

4. "Within a few days you will be baptized with the Holy Spirit. . . . You will receive power when the Holy Spirit comes upon you, and then you will be My witnesses not only in Jerusalem, but throughout Judea and Samaria, and indeed to the farthest ends of the earth." (Acts 1:5, 8)

5. When the day of Pentecost arrived, they were all assembled together in one place.

6. Suddenly, there came from heaven a sound similar to that of a violent wind, and it filled the entire house in which they were sitting.

7. Then there appeared to them tongues as of fire, which separated and came to rest on each one of them. All of them were filled with the Holy Spirit and began to speak in different languages, as the Spirit enabled them to do so.

8. Now staying in Jerusalem there were devout Jews from every nation under heaven. At this sound, a large crowd of them gathered, and they were bewildered because each one heard them speaking his own language. (Acts 2:1-6)

9. Peter answered, "Repent, and be baptized, every one of you, in the name of Jesus Christ, so that your sins may be forgiven, and you will receive the gift of the Holy Spirit. For the promise that was made is for you, for your children, and for all those who are far away, for all those whom the Lord our God will call." (Acts 2:38, 39)

10. Those who accepted his message were baptized, and on that day about three thousand people were added to their number. (Acts 2:41)

4. *The Assumption of Mary*

1. The Lord God said to the serpent, "I will establish hostility between you and the woman, and between your line and her line.

Her offspring will crush your head and you will bruise His heal." (Gen 3:15)

2. A great sign appeared in heaven: a woman clothed with the sun, with the moon beneath her feet, and a crown of twelve stars on her head. (Rev 12:1)

3. My daughter, listen carefully to my words and follow them diligently. Forget your people and your father's house; then the King will desire your beauty. Since He is your Lord, bow down before Him. (Ps 45:11-12)

4. "Blessed are you, daughter, by the Most High God, above all the women on earth."

5. "Blessed be the Lord God, the creator of heaven and earth, under whose guidance you cut off the head of the leader of our enemies. The hope that you inspired will never fade from the memory of those who praise the power of God."

6. "May God make your deed redound to your everlasting honor and shower blessings upon you, because you risked your life when our nation was facing annihilation, and you averted our ruin, walking uprightly before the Lord." (Jdt 13:18-20)

7. "You are the glory of Jerusalem, the surpassing pride of Israel, the great honor of our people. With your own hand you have done all this; you have done good to Israel, and God is

pleased with what you have wrought. May you be blessed by the Lord Almighty forever and ever!" (Jdt 15:9-10)

8.   Who is this that comes forth like the dawn, as beautiful as the moon, as resplendent as the sun, as formidable as an army with banners? (Song 6:10)

9.   "I love those who love me, and those who diligently seek me find me. . . . He who finds me finds life and wins the favor of the Lord." (Prov 8:17, 35)

10.   Mary has been taken up into heaven; the choirs of the Angels rejoice! *(Assumption)*

5. *The Crowning of Mary as Queen of Heaven*

1.   Daughters of kings are among your women in waiting; at Your right hand is Your queen adorned in gold of Ophir. . . . The king's daughter is adorned in robes threaded with gold. In embroidered garments she is led to the king; followed by her virgin companions, who are also led to You. (Ps 45:10, 14-15)

2.   My heart is moved by a noble theme as I sing my poem to the king. (Ps 45:2)

3.   You are the most handsome of men; grace has anointed Your lips, for God has blessed You forever. (Ps 45:3)

4.   I rejoice in the Lord with all my heart; my soul exults in my God. For He has clothed me in garments of salvation and wrapped me in a robe of saving justice, like a bridegroom adorned with a garland or a bride bedecked with her jewels. (Is 61:10)

5.   "My soul proclaims the greatness of the Lord and my spirit rejoices in God my Savior."

6.   "For He has looked with favor on the lowliness of His servant; henceforth all generations will call me blessed."

7.   "The Mighty One has done great things for me, and holy is His name." (Lk 1:46-49)

8.   All ages speak of your glory, O virgin Mary. Blest are you by the Lord. It is you who give us the fruit of life. *(Assumption)*

9.   The Holy Virgin was raised up, above the angels into the kingdom of heaven. *(Assumption)*

10.   In your splendor and your beauty, triumph and reign, O Virgin Mary. *(Assumption)*

PRAYER AFTER THE ROSARY

O GOD, Whose only-begotten Son, by His Life, Death, and Resurrection, has purchased for us the rewards of eternal life; grant, we beseech You, that, meditating upon these Mysteries of the Most Holy Rosary of the Blessed Virgin Mary, we may imitate what they contain and obtain what they promise, through the same Christ our Lord. Amen.

℣. May the divine assistance remain always with us. ℟. Amen.

℣. And may the souls of the faithful departed, through the mercy of God, rest in peace. ℟. Amen.